9/20/05

Dear Kim,
    Thank you for being so nice and for accepting me for who I am. I appreciate it. I wish you all the happiness and blessings in the world. Thank you for your support in the fight against ED by reading this book. I hope you enjoy it.

        God Bless!
        Autumn Christ
        a.k.a.
        Kimberly Cafe

Hiding in Plain Sight

By

Autumn Christ

1663 Liberty Drive, Suite 200
Bloomington, Indiana 47403
(800) 839-8640
www.AuthorHouse.com

This book is a work of non-fiction. Unless otherwise noted, the author and the publisher make no explicit guarantees as to the accuracy of the information contained in this book and in some cases, names of people and places have been altered to protect their privacy.

© 2005 Autumn Christ. All Rights Reserved.

No part of this book may be reproduced, stored in a retrieval system, or transmitted by any means without the written permission of the author.

First published by AuthorHouse 12/16/04

ISBN: 1-4208-2252-7 (sc)

Printed in the United States of America
Bloomington, Indiana

This book is printed on acid-free paper.

"Recovery"

© 2004 Christine Mercer-Vernon

www.mercer-vernon.com

Initially weakened by her disease, Recovery has found new strengths in herself.

Overcoming a dominating cloud of darkness, she has risen above and is walking a new road in life. Opening the door and allowing herself to be open as well, she welcomes those, still struggling, to join her on this journey. With a renewed sense of self-confidence she begins to pull herself up, stepping gingerly upon her pedestal. Though it is small, it is strong and steady and will support her as she raises her head smirking, she know who she is.

Nourishing her body and facing her reflection no longer frighten her. She carries a symbolic shield of strength and beauty and grasps her rope with pride, knowing she has the power in her to keep herself steadily climbing.

An icon of strength for those recovering from an eating disorder, Recovery knows the struggles well, but she also knows we all possess the strength to pull ourselves up out of the darkness letting light shine upon us again.

Preface

I would like to introduce myself to you, my name is Autumn, I am thirty-two years old and I suffer from an Eating Disorder. I have been battling both Anorexia and Bulimia for twenty-four years and now I am finally in recovery. I have been in a strong recovery now for four months and I look forward to continuing this.

I began when I was nine years old making myself a promise that I would never be "fat" again. The truth is, I was not fat then. I only believed I was. I began taking laxatives everyday then worked my way to restricting, purging, over exercising and ipecac. I did not know then how deadly any of this could be or how much damage I would be doing to my body.

I know now what price I have paid to be "thin" and believe me once you read a little further on you will see the price was too high. I was born with Kidney Disease and three kidneys. I am now down to one kidney and it is working well for me as of my most recent surgery in February of 2004. I also have severe Irritable Bowel Disease as well as GERD, Acid Reflux and other stomach problems due to my laxative and ipecac abuse.

The restricting, purging and over exercising added to all of this and to make matters worse my only dream has been to have children and partially due to my eating disorder, I am unable to have children also. These are all serious side effects from doing these routines to lose a few pounds and stay thin. Sad isn't it. I become speechless everyday when I find out the damage I have done to my body. I never imagined being in such bad shape medically by my own doing.

From being called a walking corpse by my doctor to being hospitalized with tubes down my throat as well as in my veins and heart monitors on me daily while in the hospital, I can honestly say was scary enough for me to wake up and finally realize that enough was enough. It is time to heal. I have to quit this behavior and recover or I am going to die.

I went to a partial hospitalization program willingly and I am glad that I did. Not only have I found a way to stop being active in my eating disorder, but I have also found a new light to write a book which will be used to help others recover and heal from eating disorders, abuse, mental illness and self-injury.

I know that not every program out there gives their patients the opportunities that I have had given to me, but I have also chosen to take it upon myself to get everything out of my stay possible to make myself well and be able to help others.

I always needed to be "thin" so I thought because I was in acting and modeling and this is what is expected from you. I have the California mentality of you are never too rich or too thin, you must look and act a certain way and a salad is considered a meal for young ladies. This is all the biggest crock I have ever heard in my life. Totally unacceptable. I lived in California born and raised for thirty-one years and now I see just how much it harmed me to have that mentality.

I have had to give up my dream of becoming a Mother one day biologically and I will never know the feeling of giving birth to a child. This hurts me more than anything in this world. I have been through so much in my life, but this is the hardest thing to imagine for myself.

I was also in an abusive relationship with my ex-boyfriend, he would hit me, smack me, bruise my face and body with severe force and trauma and also mentally abused me for ten of the twelve years we were together. I didn't stay with him because I loved him, I stayed because I was scared to leave. Afraid of what would happen if I had left. My self-esteem was so poor that I believed that I deserved to be beat around and used for a punching bag.

So eventually, I started cutting myself to release the pain of not being in control of my eating disorder, my pain, my abuse or my life. I would have to see myself bleed to feel the release of the pain I was in wash away from my body. One day I had been cutting too much and went too far. I was caught by my doctors and was committed for three days to a mental institution for cutting myself in every unimaginable place possible over one hundred times.

Those three days were the worst yet best days I have spent anywhere. I made use of the time well contemplating if I should continue cutting or finally say goodbye to all the pain once and for all. So I was released and have not cut or harmed myself since. It has now been two years and five months since I have hurt myself.

I am looking forward to my three year anniversary. I do celebrate them every month because I deserve to. I make a solemn vow to myself every month that I will stay in recovery and I will never harm myself again. Now I am also doing this with my eating disorder looking forward to my one year anniversary.

If I can prevent even one of you from doing the same things to your bodies as I have done to mine, then I have served my purpose here on earth. If you need help or know someone who does please get the help that is out there and start the healing process. You will not regret it I promise you.

I may not be skinny now or even what I want to be physically, but I am healthy, happy and have family members including my new loving Fiancé and his family to support me and live my life as I want to filled with unconditional love, respect and trust. You can too if you want it badly enough.

Introduction

I would like to first off dedicate this book to the millions of men and women who have lost their lives to Eating Disorders and to those who are battling both Anorexia and Bulimia Nervosa now. Please find your own path to recovery as it is the most important gift to give yourself. This is also dedicated to the survivors of Abuse and Rape. You are true heros for surviving your traumatic experiences.

Throughout the chapters in this book you will find stories, personal journal entries, poetry, letters written to loved ones and those who have caused their pain. You will also find insight and feedback on the creating of this book. Not everyone is happy it is being written because the blame for my illness comes out in it as well as others. The goal is to write a book which can help others in need and to help them heal. I am no longer going to hide behind my pain and fears because when you do this, all you are doing is continuing the vicious cycle and making it impossible to heal.

I apologize to anyone who cannot accept my reasons and strength for doing this book, but it is time I live my life for me and I heal as well as help others to stand up in this fight and heal as well. It takes a lot of strength to write what is published in this book and to share it is even harder to do. Please do not pass judgement on anyone in this book and do not doubt the tears and sadness that made this book possible. I sincerely thank all of you who helped me in the creation and publication of this book. I am forever truly grateful and please know you will never be forgotten for believing in me and standing by my side.

God Bless and Thank You All,

Autumn

Ed

Ed is a term that is very common when you have an eating disorder. Ed is my eating disorder and the worst man in my life. He controls me everyday and to break free from him seems impossible. I hate him because he showed up when I was nine years old. I gave myself a birthday present on my ninth birthday. I was going to be thin if it killed me. Luckily, I have not given Ed the pleasure of ending my life. Instead he has only made it a harder one to live.

I am in recovery, yet still active in my eating disorder if that makes any sense to you. I had times where I weighed almost two-hundred pounds, but there were many factors in that weight not just being fat. With all my medical conditions, I would and still do carry a lot of excess weight from water retention and bowel problems. The difference is now I may not be a hundred pounds like I want to be, but I am healthy.

I feel better physically than I ever have, my coloring is great, I have energy to do the things I want to do with moderation. That is a key word, Moderation. Everything you do in life must be done in moderation because otherwise you will kill yourself trying to do too much at one time. Overeating and over exercising are not what works.

Eating right and sensible and exercising right and sensible in moderation are what beats Ed. I may never weigh what I want to mentally be able to accept again. In the words of my dietician, You may be able to mentally accept 125 lbs., I can mentally accept being thirty but lets face it neither one can happen ever again. We are not able to do this ever again. Makes sense huh. You can't change your age, why do we try so hard to change our weight so drastically. If we are healthy who gives a damn.

The only thing that matters in this lifetime is that we are happy, healthy both mentally and physically and we are in control of our own lives. No one can make you do anything you don't want to do once you have your life straightened out. NO ONE. I am to the point now where my life is going to be one filled with all the joys and happiness God has blessed me with and I am not about to let anyone take this away from me. That includes Ed. Easier said than done, of course, but possible, definitely. I may be active in my eating disorder, but I am also active in my life and in control of my eating disorder. I am not there completely yet, but one day I will be.

I have stopped taking all the laxatives, stopped the diet pills, over exercising, purging, ipecac and other means I was using, now all I have to do is end the restricting and lack of control from letting Ed have a say in my life. He is the enemy not me. I will spend the rest of my life trying to recover and heal daily, the difference is rather than wanting to die, I want to live. I have been given so many great gifts in my life finally, I don't want to see them stop and I want to cherish every one like it is the most important one I have been given. The next time Ed tries to control me I am going to tell him to go to hell. I don't need him in my life anymore.

Sometimes we wake up in one of those moods where we just don't feel like we belong anywhere. Feeling the need to hide away from the world wishing we were invisible. Unsure of what the day may hold for us and afraid to face what may come our way. I know this sounds all too familiar to you because I still have several days like this. I want to be in a happy pleasant mood, but it just doesn't seem possible.

You get tired of the everyday life that you must deal with and not to exist you feel would be better for everyone. I know I feel like a burden to those who love me because of all the pain I have caused them. The tears they cry because of me seem to wash away all the love we have for each other.

Feeling so alone and desperate wanting someone to just put their arms around you to let you know that everything will be okay. Frustrated and angry when this doesn't happen. Feeling unloved and like no one can understand, relate or care about me the way I need them to.

Parents, family members and friends tell you to stop this behavior and yell at you thinking this will change everything. I have heard so many times these phrases. "Cut it out". "Stop being stupid" and my all time favorite "I don't like the way I look and I feel fat too, but you don't see me starving and making myself sick do you?" As if these comments help us at all. Then you get the thought in your mind that if they really believed they hated themselves as much as I hate myself they would do something about it too.

They could go on a diet, stop eating as much, cut out the fat, carbs and sugar, purge, restrict anything to make themselves look better like we do. They are just weak and they have no willpower strength or they don't care enough to change themselves. All of this is so wrong, they aren't screwed up, we are for believing body image is more important than who we are on the inside.

They have the right idea to enjoy life to the fullest and accept themselves for the genetics they have been given. Our bone structure is a major factor in the determination of how thin or heavy we will be. We can maintain a healthy weight and stay in shape but ultimately we cannot choose to all be the same build. It just isn't possible.

For example, in my family all the women have always been on the round, short and heavy end of the spectrum, but for the most part healthy. As for the men, they have always been taller, thinner and naturally more muscular. It sucks and it isn't fair but it is our genetic makeup. We all have a set point our bodies are accustomed to and will maintain if we allow it to stay healthy.

As soon as we begin the starving process and begin losing weight in one way or another unhealthily, we are slowing down our metabolism to such a bare minimum you will stop losing weight. You may even start gaining weight or retain fluid in your abdomen or other parts of your body which will make you also weigh more. This will make you want to starve yourself more, exercise more and harder, purge excessively or take more diet pills just to try and get rid of the weight you are gaining.

The problem with this is, when you do this you are slowly killing yourself causing your organs to shut down and eventually you could turn into a vegetable, have heart failure, renal failure, liver failure and finally you will die. I am not trying to scare you, I am only giving you the facts as to what happens if you continue this deadly cycle.

Anorexia Vs. Bulimia

When you compare Anorexia vs. Bulimia, there are some differences in the patters and behaviors of the eating disorders. The following pages will discuss the symptoms to look for and the difference between both disorders. Hopefully this will better educate you on anorexia and bulimia, because though the symptoms are similar there are differences that determine which you or a loved one may be suffering from. Regardless of the label help is needed and neither can be ignored.

Anorexia is a disorder where Ed tells us to starve ourselves, purge through vomiting, laxatives, enemas, suppositories, ipecac or over exercising. With anorexia the rapid loss of weight, usually several pounds, being extremely underweight, wear baggy or loose fitting clothes to hide our bodies, pale skin tone, discolored fingernail beds and eyes, amenorrhea, low potassium and phosphate levels, low body temperature(feeling cold all the time), acne, loss of hair, insomnia, depression, tooth decay or loss from the acid of vomiting and poor posture.

Rather than eating food we show the mirage of eating while we hide food, spit it out in napkins, go to the restroom very often, feed it to our pets, cut our food into tiny pieces and move it around on our plate or play with it, and finally claiming we have already eaten or are not hungry at that time when we haven't eaten and are suffering from hunger pangs.

These are some of the classic symptoms to look for or if you have them it is time to get help. There are many more and other ways to lose weight, but none of these are safe they are deadly. So if you need help or someone you know does, go at the subject carefully, but do something about it now.

Bulimia is a disorder where we tend to do some of the same habits associated with anorexia, with a difference of eating or binging on foods till we can eat no more or become sick then we purge by the same means as anorexics do. Many times we tend to be of normal weight or a higher than normal weight and look to be perfectly fine. The truth is we are just as sick as if we were anorexic. Our levels drop just as badly and are just as serious being so low because regardless of your weight if your bodies levels are off your affecting your immune system and organ functions.

The amount of acid found in our bodies with both disorders can and does cause irritation or damage to our esophagus, heartburn, acid reflux, GERD, gastrointestinal problems, bowel and stomach problems, gas and fluid retention, irritable bowel syndrome, infertility and sterility, ulcers, colitis, cancer can develop possibly, pancreatic and liver problems. There are several more conditions that can be caused by these deadly disorders.

I know that none of these medical conditions are planned or wanted, but by neglecting our bodies they can happen to us. If you do not want these conditions and diseases, we must stop ourselves from destructing in these ways. Some could cause you to have to have surgeries that are irreversible like a colostomy. Which is the removal of part of your large intestines, causing you to wear a bag on the side of your hip to dispose of your stool for the rest of your life. Many problems can occur and some are extremely more serious than others especially if left untreated.

If you are reading this book you know you are suffering from an eating disorder and need help or someone you love is sick and you are trying to better educate yourself on their disorder. Either way you are doing the right thing by finding out more and knowing it is time to get help.

I am not a physician, only a survivor of these disorders and through experiences of my own as well as countless numbers of years doing research have I found the information I am giving to you in this book. Do not use this book to diagnose or treat someone, use it as a guideline on what not to do and how to get help for yourself or the one you love in need.

Common Misconceptions

This chapter will talk about common misconceptions people have about Anorexia and Bulimia. People judge you whenever they find out you have an eating disorder. They believe that you are supposed to be either really skinny or really heavy depending on your disorder. This is a huge misconception. Just because you have an eating disorder, doesn't mean you will look a certain way or you will weigh a certain weight. Anyone can be anorexic or bulimic regardless of size. Some of the healthiest looking people have an eating disorder. At the same time these are some of the weakest and most ill victims of these disorders possible.

Our society has told us we have to look like a super model, be a size two and act like a lady in order to fit in this world today. This is so ridiculous to hear let alone to try and achieve. Why can't we just be ourselves and not go by societies stupid and impossible rules. We are not all meant to look the same or meant to be a size two. I would rather have intelligence, wisdom and a great personality rather than fight to wear the same size as everyone else and look like anyone in specific let alone generally the same. If God intended us to look identical to each other, he would have made it happen. That is the beauty about being an individual, we can be real and be who we are and though some people may not like us, others will and we can only pray that the ones we love will love us unconditionally. After all, that is the true meaning of loving and living a healthy and happy life.

Another misconception people tend to have about us is we do this for the attention. First of all the only attention we usually get is negative so why would we do this to ourselves purposely? We are the opposite, we don't want attention we want to deny everything and hide from the world. Be invisible, if you will. They think that we want to look this way whether we are skin and bones or heavy set, we don't want attention and we don't want to be stared at or even sympathy. We want to be left alone. The attention we get so often ends up putting us deeper in the cycle of our eating disorder or causes us to relapse.

Yet another misconception is that we are only doing this because it is cool or hip. This is the furthest from the truth, and if anyone is doing this they need to stop now. It is not cool or hip and the reality is the game we are playing with ourselves is Russian Roulette. Imagine if someone who didn't have an eating disorder decided to start starving themselves everyday, purging or binging, how long do you think they would think it was cool or hip. I guarantee not long if even one day. They would hate doing this, having an eating disorder is not fun, funny, cool or hip it is deadly.

We do this to ourselves because somewhere we are craving and missing the love, support, respect, self-esteem or facing traumatic issues in our lives, it is not about FOOD! When we find the root of the problems we are facing only then can we fight to change the disorder we have grown accustomed to having in our lives.

I know people make fun of us and laugh at us and they think we are funny, the truth is we aren't funny we are in serious need of help. How can anyone expect us to recover when these misconceptions cause excessive pain or trauma that cannot possibly end immediately, if at all? The only way to reach us is to give us support, unconditional love and a shoulder to cry on when it is needed. This could be everyday even several times a day.

There are so many more misconceptions which could fill a book of its own, so the next time someone misunderstands why we do what we do, tell them to become educated about your disease and tell them you need help to heal because misconception or not we are sick and we are dying everyday. Just because we aren't in a casket yet, doesn't mean we aren't dead inside. To feel this alone and embarrassed or ashamed is not what we want. What we want is to feel happy again or even for the very first time and know we are loved for who we are and not because we are a pity case. This won't end overnight or by someone telling you that you need to stop. If it were this easy no one would be going through this.

Autumn Christ

The Media

While there are many celebrities today suffering from what you and I suffer from, there are millions more unknown out there needing help who are silent. Because we are not in the spotlight of everyone's day to day media frenzy we go unnoticed, trying to find ways to receive help and are dying because we aren't financially able to receive help in time. It almost seems to me that we aren't as important as the celebrities out there. Luckily we at least have our privacy in these bad times.

This may sound cruel to say, but think about it. We fight this war just as television personalities and musicians would, but one slip of the tongue about them going into treatment or a bad picture is taken of them and they are smeared across the media and tabloids. This makes everyone suddenly notice that there are eating disorders out there and they are serious. I am starting a ribbon awareness campaign for Eating Disorder Awareness beginning October 2004. This will promote awareness about Eating Disorders and raise money to help those in need of medical treatment for their disorders who cannot afford treatment.

I want there to be help for everyone in need not just the fortunate ones like me who have medical insurance, because so many die from this disease every year and maybe if they find help before it is too late we can begin to save lives one at a time. So when you see a black and yellow ribbon please know this ribbon is for The Fight Against ED. The colors signify coming from the darkness of an eating disorder (black), into the light of recovery (yellow). The money raised from these ribbons will go to help others so please buy a ribbon and help me in this fight against eating disorders. Others will be truly grateful for your support.

Athletes and Ed

There are many sports or activities for both boys and girls that cause Ed to show himself. Anything from dancing, ice skating and cheerleading to track, swimming, wrestling, boxing, body building and horseback riding (i.e. jockeys). Sometimes we are told or conditioned to be in a certain weight class or have a specific shape or figure for the sport we are active in. Ed counts on these activities to help him gain control of his victims.

Everyday it is becoming more known to us that eating disorders in athletes exist and are getting out of control. Every sport listed above is involved and there may be others as well. We cannot allow these activities to take our lives. It is one thing to love what you are doing and becoming an outstanding athlete, but what good would our bodies be if these activities take our lives.

Just like steroids are deadly in athletes, so are eating disorders. Dehydration, ketone acidosis, temporary paralysis, low potassium and phosphate levels, poor muscle structure, arthritis, broken and weak bones as well as other medical problems can happen if we continue to be active in our eating disorders. Trust me none of these activities or sports are worth losing your life over.

I am not saying to not enjoy yourself or do what you love, I am saying to please do it safely and if it does begin to make you ill, stop and heal before you attempt to go any further. Life is more important than any sport we choose to be a part of. If you have someone pushing you to continue in these activities they need to know what is going on. You should never hide an eating disorder. Because once you begin you simply feel it is impossible to end.

There are healthy ways of becoming physically fit for these sports, so find out how to be healthy and still maintain your active role in the sport you choose. A doctor, nutritionist, dietician, coach or physical fitness trainer can give you all the information you need to do this right, so ask. Don't let anything destroy your life, especially Ed. He is the last person you will ever be able to trust in life. He is poison.

The bottom line is whether you are male or female or an amateur or professional in the sport you do, please be healthy at any cost. Your life depends on it. Ed depends on us allowing him to have control over us and believe it or not men are and always will be just as likely to have an eating disorder as a woman can be. The difference is it is not discussed or found as often.

The statistics show that one out of every ten males have an eating disorder and seven out of every ten females have an eating disorder. Regardless of the statistics, one person suffering is too many and needs to end. We cannot afford to lose lives to such a horrific and senseless disease. If more awareness about eating disorders existed, it is possible these numbers could end up being even higher than they are now. This is the reason I am trying so hard to familiarize society about eating disorders. We need to put an end to Ed once and for all.

Men vs. Women

We all have fat days, even when we are "normal." Normal meaning we do not suffer from an eating disorder. As women, we are taught we must be dainty, feminine and petite. As men, they are taught to be masculine, strong and protectors of women. The rules are different and I don't understand why. We should for the most part be treated equally. There are times when women need to be defended or protected, but for the most part we can handle ourselves pretty well. Men use their physical strength and muscle to protect us, while we use our minds to get out of dangerous situations.

Abuse or rape for example, we allow the attacker to believe he is in control because psychologically this is what he is trying to have over us not just the physical and sexual power. By allowing them to believe this we are more likely to survive the attack and be able to catch the attacker with the help of law enforcement. Once the attacker feels that he has lost control, the abuse or rape becomes more violent if not deadly for us.

Both men and women are both human, but raised completely different. While women are taught to show their emotions and feel as they do, men are taught to be strong and to never show weakness or cry. This is a double standard. Both men and women should be able to show emotions they are feeling regardless of how they choose. I would rather see a man show the emotional side than hold it inside and see them one day burst into the anger they hold within.

A woman will naturally have those all too common "fat days." Throughout life our bodies continuously go through a changing cycle. From puberty to menopause. Our bodies change from being atypical shapes and sizes to developing curves and breasts throughout the early teen and pre-teen years. Once we hit puberty, we have a menstrual cycle causing our bodies to retain water weight and have hormonal changes.

A man does go through puberty as well with physical as well as hormonal changes in their bodies, but to have the all too common "fat days" is not as common for them. They are more likely to experience a different form of feeling uncomfortable with their bodies. Their voice will change, body structure, hair growing more rapidly and certain other urges or changes occur as well.

So the next time you have a "fat day" or feel uncomfortable with your body please remember that both men and women have commonalities that make us all feel uncomfortable and Ed never helps he only harms us when we allow him to become part of our lives. Our earliest years are when he is most likely ready to pounce on us and make us feel as though we need him. Don't give in to Ed. He is and always will be the enemy in our lives.

Safe Vs. Not Safe Foods

Many people do not understand the difference between safe and not safe foods for those of us who suffer from eating disorders. The meaning of safe foods are foods we know cannot make us fat or are low enough in calories, fat, sugars and carbohydrates that cannot possibly harm us. Not safe foods are those foods that "normal" everyday people don't worry about let alone think to be okay for them to eat.

Safe foods are foods like salads with no dressing or fat free dressing(lettuce), vegetables plain or raw, fat free crackers, water, diet sodas, chicken, fish or turkey(grilled not fried) and condiments like mustard or ketchup. Anything that is roughage and can leave our bodies quickly without the ability to store fat, sugar or carbs is considered to be safe. Some candies like gummy bears or sweedish fish(only a few) or sugar free jello and broths are also on the safe list.

Everyone who suffers with an eating disorder has a different safe food list they go by. The individual chooses what is safe and what is not. For me my safe foods are lettuce, carrots, celery, greens, wheat or no salt crackers, sugar free jello, water and pure juice with all natural sugars. Bread was never safe. I have allowed myself no more than five to ten grams of fat per day, twenty to thirty carbs, and about two to five hundred calories a day depending on my mood.

Most of the time my diet consisted of pure liquids because there is no substance to the calories and they cannot make you fat. If it didn't need to digest it was perfect. Another safe food was anything I would chew a bite of a few times then spit out in a napkin. I couldn't allow myself to swallow my food or I would have to purge it up immediately.

I was never someone who would binge, I always restricted and purged whether it be by using laxatives, enemas, ipecac, vomiting or over exercising. Now that I am in recovery I have been able to see how terribly I treated my body and how wrong I have been for so long about my safe food list. You never think about how stupid or sick you are when you are active in your eating disorder all you care about is what Ed tells you to do.

I now reward myself on rare occasions when I have done really well in my recovery by allowing myself one of my not safe foods from before. My weakness has always been cheesecake and I hope that one day I will again be able to be brave enough to try a bite. For now, I am too afraid of it and do not allow anything close.

I still count everything and even though my nutritionist wants me to be up to a minimum of one-thousand to twenty-eight hundred calories a day, I am still well under the minimum. I am eating, just small quantities, low calorie, low fat, low carb and low sugar foods. Usually I have four to six mini meals a day to help adjust my body to eating again and to speed up my metabolism. I have my bad days and the past few days I have been very vulnerable with some restricting, the difference is now I am aware of it and I ask for support from my family to help me fight against Ed. I said before I have a long way to go and I am not perfect or totally recovered. The important thing is I have not purged in any way and will not allow myself to do so.

I live my life through my recovery remembering everyday is a new day and tomorrow can and will be better for me. I just continue to try harder and stay in touch with my support team and talk to them about how I have done each day. It helps me and it lets them know I am doing okay.

Holidays

Every year we celebrate holidays with platters and bowls filled with food. I don't know of a harder way to celebrate the holidays for someone with an eating disorder. Society believes you must get fat and full during the holidays I guess. Think about it, every holiday big or small seems to revolve around food. Beginning with New Year's Day throughout the year till Christmas.

Why are we so obsessed with feeding our faces and seeking out an excuse to celebrate food rather than the true meaning of the holiday at hand. I am not saying it is bad to eat because we must have food to survive, but there are so many ways to celebrate the holidays without worrying ourselves with what to cook and how much to have on each occasion.

I dread every holiday because I am so scared of what is expected of me to eat. Those who know about my eating disorder, understand that I will fix a plate with what I feel is reasonable for me. If I am caught slacking, I am told to get a little more. For the most part I am getting better throughout my recovery thankfully.

The best way to make it through this scary time is to look at what others eat and try to attempt some of the same foods, just much smaller portions. I usually take the serving size that a young child would eat at first, and if I feel safe and able to have a little more without making myself sick I will a few hours later. I space out my eating so I can stay strong in recovery, yet make myself and others proud of my accomplishments.

You must retrain your body to eat and keep down your food. It may not work for everyone to do as I do, but it works well for me. I also feel more confident and comfortable around my family during the holidays now, because I know by doing this I am the one in control not Ed. I enjoy myself now so much more than I ever have and at the end of the celebration I can say I ate and behaved like a "normal" person.

"Triggered Feelings Raining Down"

© 2004 Christine Mercer-Vernon

www.mercer-vernon.com

Feelings of inadequacy, loss of control, sadness, depression, anxiety, wanting to be accepted, wanting to be perfect, wanting to beautiful, hating myself, hating my reflection….. Sometimes they come out of nowhere, raining down on me, beating hard on my shoulders. Sometimes I cry, sometimes I go completely numb. Brought on by so many things. Why do I have to feel this way?

Triggers

There are so many things that can trigger us in our eating disorders and self-injury. They can be simple things like seeing an old friend, a class reunion, date, dance, job, family member, food, emotion, even a color or the way something or someone smells. The wind can blow in the wrong direction and it could trigger us.

When it is sunny, bright and absolutely beautiful outside we may be in a happy and strong mood. But if it is dark, raining, dreary or gloomy outside we may want to isolate ourselves where you and Ed have too much free time on your hands. Karen Carpenter had a song called "Rainy days and Mondays". This song is a major trigger for me especially on the rainy or snowy winter days in the fall and winter time.

I feel so depressed, sad, lonely, trapped and empty inside. I dread getting up in the morning because I know Ed is home and waiting to tell me how to spend my day. So I begin by turning on music, begin to cry feeling ashamed and guilty because of how much my eating disorder affects me and everyone around me.

I feel like I ruin everything. I have nowhere to turn and no one to turn to except for Ed. He will take care of me, protect me, guide me and make me feel whole again. So I begin with breakfast. I find anything and everything that sounds good to me or is just simply food. Ed tells me to eat, eat, eat, more, more, more, faster, shovel it in "fill our hunger." Then he says you are so weak, I tricked you fatty, you are ugly, hideous and disgusting. You are a monster. How could you have done this to yourself?

So you know what comes next. A finger or your whole hand down your throat just to get every bite, every calorie out of your body. You knew better than to eat like that but you just couldn't resist. So as you are heaving and purging you swear you will never eat again. Your stomach is turning, aching, cramping and you want the pain to stop.

Sometimes the pain is so bad you pass out unable to control your body. Many times this had happened to me from the laxative abuse. The day continues this way for lunch, dinner and snack times. This is the wretching disease of Bulimia taking its toll on you. You have no control and you need help but how can you ask someone for help when you are doing this to yourself.

They will think you are crazy, insane and won't like you anymore. Even worse, if you stop and gain weight they won't want to be your friend, you will be heavier than they are and you won't be cool if you can't share each others clothes. No one wants "Fatty" for a friend.

Sounds like a Catch 22 doesn't it. For example, if you have money you don't need it, but if you need it you can't get it. Classic feelings. We all want what we can't have until we have it, then we don't want it anymore. Friends, relationships, cars, clothes whatever. Once the newness wears off who cares about it?

An eating disorder never gets old because we gain something from it. The habits get old but the disorder does not. We gain beauty, shapely curves, even perfection. Everything we need to make our lives the way we want them to be. I now see how trapping this disorder is. You live, you suffer, you die. That simple.

Where does being yourself, being human, happy and successful come in? Nowhere. You miss out on everything your life can be by depriving yourself of everything you want. The true meaning of diet to me is you die trying to deprive yourself of everything that will or can make you happy in life. I don't want this to be my life anymore. I want to be free and content being myself and enjoy everything this world has to offer me.

Take a moment and write down your triggers and next to them write down what happens when they occur. Then read over them and try to find ways to have positive reactions to them. If you work hard on this every trigger you have can and will slowly disappear.

This is not an exercise that I have been told to do, this is just the way I have found works for me to be able to heal and help with my triggers. It somehow seems to ease my mind and my urges to binge, purge, restrict, take diuretics and over exercise.

If it doesn't help you then you have lost nothing, but if it does help you, you will have gained recovery. I hope this works for you as well as it has for me. I am no longer on medications for my eating disorder because first of all they don't seem to help me and second, I am more alert, aware and stronger in my recovery than I have ever been.

I still have bad days, but the best therapy for me is finding ways to help others. I don't want to be rich or have all the materialistic possessions in the world. I want to know I have made a difference in someone else's life. One or one million, the more the better. This is my happiness, my goal, my freedom and my reward.

Autumn Christ

Laxative Abuse

Laxatives and diuretics are just as bad for you as restricting and vomiting are, if not worse. They are stimulants that overwork your kidneys, stomach, bowel, liver, colon, intestines and heart as well as other organs. In other words they are deadly. I have been addicted to laxatives, suppositories, enemas, diuretics or water pills and diet pills such as ephedrine for twenty-four years. I have seriously damaged my body over this length of time and the damage that has been done is now irreversible. I am not proud of myself in fact I am embarrassed and ashamed of what I have done to my body for so long.

I was blessed with the miracle of life and now the opportunity to create a life has been taken from me. I took for granted the gift my Mother and God gave to me and I have been trying to figure out what I have done that has been so unforgivable to not deserve to have a child until this minute.

I destroyed my precious gift of life that has been given to me and my karma is being unable to conceive a child. Funny thing about karma, you never know how you will be paid back until it hits you where you live. My devastating nightmare is to be unable to live my dream of being a Mother and now this nightmare is coming true.

This hurts so bad having to realize and accept that I have caused my own fate of infertility. My heart aches like a knife is going through it. I never knew how detrimental laxatives and diuretics were or I never would have done this to myself. If you are using them please I beg of you stop immediately. I don't want anyone ending up as I have and lose their dreams because of weight issues. Life is too short and full of so much happiness if you just search and find what you are looking for and find who you are as a person.

Over Exercising

Exercising or working out is a good healthy thing to do to keep yourself in shape. However, over exercising does nothing more than harm you. The best fitness trainers in the world are for the most part sensible on their training regimens. Doctors will tell you that moderate exercise is necessary to live a healthy life, the key word being moderate. No more than an hour a day three to four times a week is necessary to stay in shape and become healthy. I used to hide everything I did from my family and friends when it came to my exercising. I would spend three to four hours a day sometimes everyday in a gym, pool, my room doing cardio or at a school running the track.

I ended up eating away the needed body fat when I did this because I was restricting, purging and doing all the other bad things at the same time. I ended up having acidosis which is where your body has no fat to burn so it burns muscle instead as fuel for it to survive. Big mistake. I lost everything that was good and turned my body into a sickly machine which no longer functioned appropriately. My fingers, hands, legs, feet, toes and arms just about every part of my body would also go numb and tingle from pins and needles going through me it seemed. I was in a state of shock I guess you could say because my body would not function the way it should have because it wasn't getting anything it needed to survive properly.

Early on this summer, I was playing basketball at a park with my Fiancé, Father-in-law and Stepson when suddenly I fell having no feeling in my upper or lower extremities. I didn't know what to do, I was so embarrassed about this that I just laid there laughing at myself hoping no one would notice what was going on. They did. I was busted. They all knew I was up to no good with my old tricks again.

My Father-in-Law wanted to kick me in the ass so bad. He gave me hell for a long while because I was being so stupid harming myself in this way. A week later I was placed in the partial program at the hospital. This was a scary episode because I had finally realized that I was literally dying slowly. My body was giving up on me and I was the cause of the pain I was suffering from doing all the things I shouldn't have been doing.

I would also have sharp pains in my chest, as if I were having a heart attack. I couldn't breath and the pains would be so severe, I didn't know what to do. I hid it until I went to the doctor and finally told them what was going on. I had been taking ipecac and ephedrine to help lose weight and purge again. I was unaware that these two drugs could cause heart failure which people die from all the time. I wasn't trying to kill myself, I only wanted to be thin. This had to stop I didn't want to die and I was headed in that direction.

After some testing, I found there was nothing wrong with my heart, I just needed to start taking better care of myself and stop this behavior. Shortly after is when I decided to go into recovery. I am now happily in recovery and proud that I have made this choice and so is my family. I love them for giving me all their support and tough love.

The body is a weird thing, we think we can handle anything and take our bodies for granted, but we just can't. It will eventually quit functioning and with no warning sometimes. My body gave me plenty of warning but I didn't want to listen to the signs. Now with one kidney I am finally listening to my body because if I don't I can and will die. I have too much to live for now and I refuse to let this happen anymore. I want to heal and repair my body so we can live a long happy life together. After all you only receive one in your life, you may as well make it as healthy as you can.

Relapse

A relapse in your recovery can happen at anytime. It is unfortunately common to have one or more relapses before you fully heal. The reason seems to me from my experience could be anything from a traumatic episode happening in your life or the memories of a traumatic experience to a specific trigger you thought you had overcome. A new stress in your life with a troubled relationship, a death or illness in your family or circle of friends or just simply Ed's voice coming back to haunt you.

I would like to say that it doesn't happen often, but my experience is it does. The truth is in some way or form most of us will have a relapse small or large. The key is to find a way to get back on track and regain your strength and courage to heal.

I have found that joining or creating a support group is a good way to find inner strength. Others can make a significant difference in your own recovery. I have a wonderful support group now which is and always has been my family. They may not be able to relate or understand fully what I have or am going through completely, but they love me unconditionally and accept me for who I am with all my imperfections.

Imperfections are our special characteristics which make us who we are. They could be small or large, but without them we are not ourselves. I also have been doing research and have found that there is a website which has support groups in our areas that meet on a monthly basis. I am the organizer for the Harrisburg and Hershey, Pennsylvania Chapter.

As of right now there are very few members and we have not held any meetings as of yet, but I plan on doing what I can to begin the meetings and find others in need so they may join and begin to heal. I am also the organizer for the Depression group in the same areas. We have more members in this group but are always looking for more to join. It only takes once a month to spend time with finding ways to heal or just simply finding strength in each other. If you are interested in joining a chapter in your area go to http://meetup.com and find out more.

I have found that it is the little things you do in life that can make a difference in someone else's life. Just think if every person in the world were to do one small yet important thing for another person what a difference we could make in this world for ourselves and our children. I may be dreaming about this ever truly happening but I believe most anything is possible to a certain extent. I have a friend named Sara who brought over a movie one day for me to watch called "Pay It Forward."

This movie is about what I have been describing above and this movie reinforced that I am not the only one who dreams about this miracle happening. I am paying it forward to you by writing this book and trying to help you heal in return for so many people helping me in my recovery. Friends, family members, doctors and you.

Here is an exercise for you to try if and when you feel a relapse coming on. Try and think of one thing you can do to help someone else. At the same time let it be something that will help you as well. Big or small doesn't matter. What matters is you keep yourself occupied and your mind on something other than your disorder. This can help for any addiction, disease or disorder out there. Not just Ed.

Whether you succeed in helping that person or not is ultimately irrelevant, what is important is that you heal and find a way to think of others as well as loving yourself. The worst that can happen is you find it didn't work. The best that can happen is you have helped someone else and recovered from your disorder at the same time.

There have been several times in my previous as well as present recovery where I have felt a relapse coming on. My doctors are worried and concerned about me now because they believe I am having a Manic episode. I am obsessing over this book so I can meet my deadline and I am depriving myself of sleep so that I can complete it. What they don't realize is this is the first time I have been this excited about anything this important in my life and I want to attain my goal.

This book is therapy for me and is working beautifully. I feel stronger, more energized, healthier and more proud of myself now than I ever have in my life. I am achieving recovery and helping others hopefully at the same time. I am not concerned with the time I am spending now on this project because once it is done, I will take the time to rest and take care of myself the way I need to. I am only praying that once I am done, I am able to continue my recovery as strong as I am now.

I am on the best and only high for me, a natural high. Happy I am succeeding and glad that things are going so smoothly with this book. I am putting myself first in my life with my recovery for the first time in my life and secondly I am being honest with myself and others by achieving my goal of helping others.

Autumn Christ

Partial Hospitalization

I was in a partial hospitalization program for about nine weeks and this is where I began finding myself. I found myself by seeing other young ladies, women and men whom were and are suffering with Anorexia and Bulimia Nervosa. This scared me so much. In the beginning it was all about feeling like I was the biggest one in our group. How could I become smaller and thinner than they were? Then it hit me just how sick I was being so thin and how sick I was with my levels being so low and uncontrolled. I found myself worrying terribly about the others in my group and wanted to find a way of spending the thirty-one hours a week there helping them if I could and in turn help myself to recover.

I would tell them my story and make them realize how serious this was. It broke my heart to see the other patients especially the younger ones doing these things and having no idea how much trouble they were getting themselves into. I wanted to help. I had to help! ... But how? What could I do to make them heal and heal myself at the same time?

Then suddenly in the middle of group, I told everyone that I had been hiding more than two hundred laxatives from everyone and I decided to throw them down the toilet and flush them. I found that leading by example may be the only way I could help others. Maybe since I am unable to have children, I can take them under my wing and try to help them recover and want to get better. I don't know if I helped them, but now I am trying to continue by helping you.

I can only pray that I did help at least one. If so, then this was the reason I was meant to be in this program and I spent the last twenty-four years slowly attempting suicide with fail. I am here to help others and that is what my mission is. I will spend the rest of my life from here on trying to do so in a positive fashion.

"Road to Recovery"

© 2004 Christine Mercer-Vernon

www.mercer-vernon.com

    Recovering from an eating disorder is a like traveling a road plagued by drastically changing weather. Full of twist and turns, it's not an easy road to navigate. Crippling lightening, blinding darkness, storms that occur spontaneously above jagged mountains. Around the bend there are sloping hills and warm sunshine where, sometime, you can lie in the fields and relax, self-assure. Occasionally, the storms sneak up on you, but if you stay on the road, keep your head up and step steadily along, trust that the clouds will part. Because, even with all the dark and dreary moments, there is hope that the sun will shine again, just around the bend.

Recovery

There are many ways to recover. The difficult choices are what scares us away from healing. Some ways may require our bodies to go through withdrawals. Whether it be from diet pills, laxatives, ipecac, pure ephedrine or other diuretics we may use to lose weight.

Stopping the purging cycle makes us feel as if we will explode from all the food (no matter how little) there may be in our system. One day at a time hell, you are lucky to get through one minute at a time, but it can be done. There is hope if you can find the strength to hold on and truly want to heal.

Binging is yet another part of these horrible disorders. Sometimes the biggest side effect it seems from anorexia is the binging. We hear things like "it is okay to eat", "don't worry about the small weight gain", "Everything will be fine" or "You need to gain some weight to become healthy again." I am sure that these all sound too familiar to you.

The way I know this is because I have been there far too many times myself. You see recovery does sometimes mean you will have a relapse along the way. I have had several relapses and still fight daily to keep them from getting the best of me.

When we binge, purge, restrict, use laxatives, diuretics, over exercise or just simply forget to eat. Either way we are killing ourselves slowly and one day we will eventually die from this disorder. I wish I could tell you that recovery has a miracle cure, but it simply doesn't. You must have the willpower to use all your strength you have used in the past to starve yourself and lose weight, to heal and believe me it is harder than anything you will ever face in your life.

I can tell you Journaling or poetry writing, as well as other outlets do work, but you have to want them to. My way of recovering is, was and will continue to be writing this book for you, helping others, counseling and using the love and support of my family and friends to get through this pain and daily struggle.

I am far from "Cured" and don't believe in preaching to get my point across, but I will and do gladly spend my time telling others who want to heal and are willing to listen about the price I have paid to "BE THIN." You may never love yourself completely or be happy with the way you look, but hopefully this will allow you to find peace within and accept yourself for who you are and not what you have or how you look. At thirty-two years old, I have one Kidney left, Irritable Bowel Disease as well as other abdominal and digestive problems, GERD, Acid Reflux, constant Heartburn, Infertility, Depression, Obsessive Compulsive Disorder and other medical illnesses which can never be repaired.

I can blame only a percentage of some of these conditions to the fact that I was born with them. However, I can blame the Anorexia as a child and adolescent and Bulimia as an adult for the twenty-four years of damage I have caused myself. I had to first and foremost admit to myself that I had been the cause of so much damage before I could even begin to want or start to heal myself.

Psychological Disorders

This chapter will talk about Psychological Disorders. There are so many of them to discuss and there are books strictly on these disorders out there for you to receive more information. I am including this chapter in this book to help familiarize some of them that associate with Eating Disorders, Abuse, Self-Injury and Rape or Molestation.

There is Depression, Multiple Personality Disorder(MPD), Obsessive Compulsive Disorder(OCD), Manic Depressive Disorder, Post Traumatic Stress Disorder(PTSD) and many more. One thing they seem to have in common are the ways they affect our lives when we associate them with these disorders. Some can be very minimal while others are more extreme.

I am no doctor, if I were though, I would try and cure Psychological Disorders. They may not be diseases like Cancer, Aids or Diabetes, but they are silent killers just the same. There are children, adolescents and adults suffering from these disorders who have attempted if not committed Suicide, Self-Injury and/or Overdosing. Because of the pain and disorder being so serious we lose lives everyday from them. To me there are lives to save and the sooner the better.

There must be a way to protect and treat these victims of disease as well. We tend to live inside our minds sometimes, rather than face or live in reality and this makes us become a prisoner in our own twisted way inside our minds and lives. We are not criminals we are sick and need help. The sad reality is most of us do not even realize it until it is too late if at all.

If you suffer from Psychological Illnesses, please get treatment. If you cannot afford it there are some organizations that can help you, the state you live in may have programs, Social Security and Medicare can help, there are ways if you want help to get it. Please do. You aren't crazy because you need help you are crazy if you don't get it, especially if you have someone medically willing to help you as well as financially.

I would have been a fool if I didn't take advantage of the medical insurance and doctors I have been blessed with to help me. No one is out to harm me, I can see this now. They are trying to make me well and I greatly appreciate it. So please do the same and begin to feel the difference in yourself. It is worth the chance you take.

Obsessive Compulsive Disorder

With Obsessive Compulsive Disorder you will find yourself cleaning too much, doing different things over and over again, you have to have everything in a specific order and basically it seems like you drive everyone around you nuts. I have been suffering from OCD for about fifteen years now. I guess it comes from all the panic attacks and anxiety that I go through on a daily basis. It happens when I begin having flashbacks, when my mood changes, if I get nervous or something happens that I get excited or scared about. Like when I found out this book was really going to happen, I started cleaning and typing so much my hands were numb.

We obsess over different things in our lives, mine deal with Ed, wanting to have a career, wanting to help others and my health. I want to be healthy and okay again. You see there are many different things that we obsess over and it amazes me how many of them are things we cannot change or just don't seem to make happen. I want to be happy, healthy, help others heal from their Eating Disorders and I would like to be married to the man I love and have children with him of our own to share in the joy of motherhood as well as see my stepson grow to be a successful and handsome young man.

I have a beautiful Niece who I adore but lives so far away. I sometimes obsess over her because I want such a wonderfully blessed life for her too. I love her just as I would my own daughter. As you can see there is nothing you cannot obsess over. There are triggers everywhere, the key is to try and calm the obsessive urges and eliminate the triggers just like anything else.

Medical Physicians and Psychiatrists can and do give you medications for this disorder. They can range from anti-depressants, psycho tropic, and anti-anxiety medications. The facts are some work and some don't. For me they don't and the one that does won't be prescribed to me because it is a dangerous medication. So I tend to deal with my OCD in a different manner. I write or tell my Fiancé to stop me when I begin to clean obsessively. I have to be clean at all times and our house must be clean at all times as well. It can be 5 a.m. and I will clean for hours or do laundry.

If you feel you may have OCD then talk to your doctor. They can help you. First they will examine you and review your history and symptoms, then they will diagnose you and treat you. We think it is hard on us, but believe me it is just as hard on the people around us because they cannot understand or relate to it.

Post Traumatic Stress Disorder

Post Traumatic Stress Disorder (PTSD) is a psychological illness that happens to us as a result of stress, trauma both physical and mental, abuse or even pregnancy. There are so many different circumstances that can cause this disorder. Your mind can block out the cause of this disorder for a matter of days, months or even years.

I have been suffering from PTSD for several years due to the traumas I have faced throughout my life. Nothing could scare me or cause me mental pain for years I believed. Why? Because my mind would block it all out so I could not be harmed. I didn't want to face all the torture and agony I had been through. I to this day am still trying to hide from my biggest fears. I have always felt that my eating disorder has helped me stay sane.

I could never have been more wrong. The only sanity to find in order to ease my pain is to admit to the trauma and abuse that has happened to me. I see a psychiatrist as well as a therapist now willingly without fail. Something I never did before. I always believed they were out to harm me and based on my previous experiences, this had always been the case.

I have found a handful of wonderful specialists in the field of psychology who have made a remarkable difference in my life. I have spent so many years being able to see the abuse, eating disorder symptoms and existing medical illnesses that I never believed they could one day ease and I could feel safe or secure again. It is going to take several more years to be able to recover from everything I have been through. I wouldn't be in my fourth month of recovery feeling so positive, if it weren't for the staff at Hershey Medical Center. Their Partial Hospitalization Program and their personal as well as professional care they continuously give to me.

I know if I relapse one more time, I most likely will not live to see who I can become one day. Knowing this and knowing that God has given me this last chance bringing me from California to Pennsylvania to heal. I will not let him, my family or myself down. I have been one of the fortunate ones to be on a strong path to recovery and if anything is meant to happen to take my life, it will not be by my doing.

This book and my passion to help others heal are how I want to be remembered when I die. We all make a mark on this world and have a specific impact on those around us. My impact and my contribution is to finish this book so you have the opportunity to learn from my mistakes and help others to recover one day at a time.

Please take what little wisdom I have and use it to your advantage so that you can help another person in need in one way or another. This way you can make your contribution too.

Psychiatric Stay

People have misconceptions about a "so-called vacation." Going to the psychiatric unit of a hospital or a psychiatric hospital period is NOT a vacation. It is hell with four walls and a big gate! I was admitted for three days against my will also known as a 5150 in California and let me tell you it was horrible.

I was sent there because of cutting myself more than a hundred times all over my body and for restricting and purging. I refused to eat and if I was made to I would purge it instantly. The cutting was totally out of control. I had so many cuts on every part of my body (literally every part). I was a freaking nightmare. I looked like a cutting board worn out from head to toe and everywhere in between was cut. It would burn every time water or sweat would come near the open wounds. I was in so much pain but I just couldn't stop.

I needed to feel the release. Even when I was being restrained and double restrained, I would make them bleed even more. I needed the release of the anger and pain eating me alive inside. I remember showering and the water making me scream in pain. It felt like salt in my wounds. I would still wait for them to scab then pick them so I could feel the release and see the blood (the pain) run from my body again. I was bandaged so I could not get to them and yet I did somehow.

I went from cutting for the release to being locked up unable to cut having to find new ways to release the pain and anger inside. I would find anything including the bed, my fingernails anything that would cause more cuts. I guess when you are that screwed up you will find a way if you want the pain to leave your body bad enough. And I did. I wanted to find some way to forget the past and I would do whatever it took to do so. I wish I could say it helped, but it just didn't. I went from having few scars from my surgeries to several on my body from cutting myself. The worst scars are those hidden to everyone but me. I think back now and know that I was doing wrong, the difference is then I just didn't care.

At meal and snack times, I would not eat. I would put food in my mouth when they were watching as if I were eating, then spit it out in the napkin or my hand and throw it into the trash can behind me. I always sat next to the trash so they would not know that I was discarding my food. They let me get by with staying in my room or shall I say my cell for the first day without getting out of bed. Why I don't know, I think they were trying to let me get adjusted to my new home. They wanted me to settle down too because I had kicked, hit, fought, scratched and kneed my way out of my restraints twice.

The Dr.'s (QUACKS) and staff (IDIOTS) even when they were shooting me in my ass with needles full of tranquilizing medicine, it only seemed to piss me off more. They couldn't calm me down. Hell I almost escaped twice when some guy helped me by causing a scene when he hit a wall and started throwing the staff against the walls. I ran. I had only one door left when I got cracked in the jaw with that door by security. So much for escaping.

I was transported to another facility from the first hospital to a more secure and stable hospital designed for so called "people like me," whatever that meant. Four in the morning and I was being transported and delivered like a slab of meat to a new place that I would be calling home for a longer period of time. That morning and every morning after they would have a freaking ritual. Wake us up at 6 a.m., stick us with a needle for blood testing for our levels and to make sure that we didn't have illegal drugs in our systems. Then came the pee test, for the same reasons. Finally we got our medications. They tried to make us all drugged up so they could have control over us at all times.

Last but not least we had a break. Fifteen minutes was the max and you could smoke if you wanted to but you couldn't bring your own with you, you had to smoke theirs and let me tell you they were freaking horrible. The worst part of the cigarettes was you begged for them like a crack head needing a quick fix. You were lucky if you got two cigarettes per break with a total of four breaks a day. That pissed me off enough to want to hit someone right there alone.

We had to go outside (which we craved) to spend time walking around the basketball courts or sitting in the sun and listening to music for about an hour a day. The rest of the time we were treated like babies. We had to take a nap in the morning after we had our break and we did our morning shower rituals. I wasn't allowed to shave and that irritated the hell out of me. I always shave and to not be able to just pissed me off more once again. I was able to wear my own clothes if I had them brought in which I did, I didn't want to walk around with my ass showing out of the back of one of their gowns.

This was a co-ed floor and believe me that didn't sit well with me. I hated having to share my space with anyone especially men. They were the reason I was in here. The cause of all my pain and here I am stuck with the looniest of them and seeing my past all around me. I had friends when I went in the hospital but after I came out, I had so few I could count them on one hand. Still can. They were the true friends that showed me what it meant to be loved for who I am and were there for me when I needed them.

Day three finally came and I was released. I had to play the game first and be able to play twenty questions in order to leave. So I did. I answered all the questions they wanted the answers to (they wanted you to screw up) but because I was observant and didn't ever lose touch with reality completely I was able to play their game and win. I left after signing my life away for so many things. No gun for five years. I was certifiable. I had been diagnosed as paranoid and delusional. The saddest part was that when I got to go home it was back to where my reality was and that just made me want to go back to hell (the psych ward) because I knew Ed would be there waiting for me with open arms. I could see that I was still out of control. I needed their help after all.

I can say that this was the longest and worst three days for me, but I can also say that those three days I spent there were for the best. My Mother and my family stood by my side. I met my Fiancé a month later and his family shortly after and the rest is history. I haven't cut since and pray that I never do again. This September 2004 will be two years and five months in recovery for self-injury (cutting). I am far from recovery, but thankfully closer to having a better and more "normal" life. I thank my family here in Pennsylvania for all they have done since I have been here and my Mother for standing by my side through my difficult times.

I won't say the urges aren't there to cut or harm myself, but I can say that I know am able to stay strong and stay in control of them and I refuse to injure or mutilate my body anymore. I have the power to write this book rather than cut myself. This way I am not only helping myself but others and together we can heal and recover. That to me is winning over the silver blade and becoming successful. I am a fighter and I am fighting to win the biggest prize of all…….. MY LIFE!!

This has been my own personal opinion and experience regarding my psychiatric stay, and is not intended or found to be the opinions of others who have been hospitalized. When hospitalization is required, take with you the hope of healing and recovery knowing you will be in safe and competent hands. The staff will be strict and the facility will be very structured, but please know it is for your best interest.

Many who go into hospitalization programs come out finding that they have succeeded in their recovery or have gained the strength to heal. Learning techniques to help you recover is what we need to find ourselves. Through our experiences in life we find wisdom to accept our faults and regain our self-esteem and confidence. Hospitalization will not harm you, it will only be a stepping stone to finding out who you are and what you can become.

Abuse

There are many forms of abuse which we have been subjected to in our lives. Whether it be physical, sexual, rape, incest, emotional or mental abuse it has taken a harsh toll on us and caused us a great deal of pain. I know that this is something that not only is hard enough to work through at the time it is happening, but the aftermath is even harder. We must choose to try and find a way of coping, working through the memories of the abuse and heal from the pain and torture we have endured. People say things "like it happened and now you have to get over it" or "forget it and move on with your life". The hard truth is you can't do it the easy way because there isn't an easy way to get over or through it. The only way is harder than most anything you have dealt with in your life.

This chapter is going to tell you some sad but true facts about what abuse can do to you. It changes your life forever with no way back to letting you see who or what kind of person you could have been had this not happened to you to begin with. I am going to give a history of abuse written by Sapphire to help you see you are not alone. I know the hardest step in trying to face the abuse is having to talk about it or share it with another soul. I am going to help you if I can to ease some of that pain by sharing a story that is very traumatic for Sapphire. She is someone who is helping to write this book with me and I want her to know how much I appreciate her for sharing her story with me and the rest of you.

I want you to know that if you have been keeping abuse a secret from someone, now is the time to open up and tell someone that can help stop it immediately. Why should we give our abusers that much power. They don't deserve it and definitely are not worth more than we are, so please tell someone. It doesn't matter who, what matters is that the abuse stops immediately.

Call a help line, tell a teacher, tell a friend, parent just please tell someone. Make the pain stop. If you are scared I understand, our abuser or attacker will say things like "if you tell you will lose your family" or "it is our little secret", "no one will believe you anyway" or any excuse to keep you from opening your mouth and getting help. To hell with all of them. You need to let someone know otherwise the abuse may not ever end and you will never begin to heal. Here is Sapphire's story.

I went through it for twelve years never telling a soul until it almost took my life. I was sexually abused and molested by my biological Father for twelve years. I was told that it was "our little secret", "it is something that happens to all your friends by their Father", "your boyfriend when you get older will appreciate this because you can show him that you know what you are doing" or the one that sticks out in my mind most was when I was told "I knew you were going to be a girl and I wanted to marry you when you got old enough".

These are things I was told everyday. I never told anyone because the biggest saying was a threat. "I will tie up your Brother, Mother, you and myself (meaning him) and I will shoot us all, you last so you can watch us all die if you ever tell anyone". This would scare anyone enough not to tell on them.

I was finally to the breaking point one evening and so I called a friend of mine. She was my best friend and I finally told her everything. She then told me I needed to tell, but I was terrified to do so. So when I went to school the next morning, she met up with me like always and said my psychology teacher wanted to see me.

I didn't think anything of it so I said okay and we went to see her. When I got there she started asking me all kinds of questions about home and what went on there. I knew that my best friend had told her about it now. I could feel that I was in trouble. I really wasn't though she was trying to help me, both of them were.

The next step was going to see the school Nurse. I wasn't as comfortable talking to her so I froze up scared to say anything about what was going on. But eventually it all came out and about three hours later I was in my counselors office. Along with two police officers and everyone telling me they were there to help me. They started asking me questions and wanting me to describe in horrific detail what had happened by him and why I hadn't told anyone. After a couple more hours it was finally lunch time. I was then taken out of school in the middle of lunch by police with handcuffs on me through the front doors of the school to a police car waiting for me. Talk about scared. I thought I was the victim not a suspect. They were afraid I would run or harm myself I was later told. Hence the reason for the handcuffs.

While I was at the school my Mother was called and told to meet us at the school, I was okay but I needed to have her with me. So once she got there she followed us to the hospital. I wasn't allowed to speak with her because they didn't want me to tell her anything at that point. I was then taken to the county hospital by my house for a rape kit test to be performed. Of course nothing would show up and I was then wondering if I had lost my mind, but the truth is I had been made to douche' for so many years and the night before this all as well, there was no semen or anything to tie him to this. I was just going through the luck of my screwed up life. I knew what had happened. My Mother told me why I would make up such a lie and what did he do to cause me to say terrible things like this. She didn't want to believe any of this was true.

I told her "Mommy it is the truth, Daddy has been doing this to me for a long time but he would kill us if I ever told you". I know she was in shock and didn't believe what I was saying, but I never lied about any of it. I wish it would have all been a nightmare that I had but it simply was the truth. I never wanted to hurt my Mother.

I have to tell you about this so you are aware that others go through this and you have to tell someone and get help if this is or has happened to you. I don't care if it was just one time or repeatedly going on please get help. I thank Autumn for allowing me to share my story with you and for writing this book.

Finally we get to the police station near my house and I was being interrogated it seemed like. They locked my Mother and I in a room together so I could tell her what was going on. All the while they were trying to contact my Father and get him to come in. He had called because he didn't know where my Mother or I was and he was scared something had happened. He was right something did happen, he was busted. They told him that he needed to come into the police station and he could pick us up. So he did. Only picking us up wasn't the plan. Arresting his ass was. I was hearing him from the room screaming and yelling trying to fight a losing battle. I was scared then. I didn't know what he was going to do. My Mother then went to talk to him and of course he denied the whole thing.

That night my Aunt and Uncle's ended up being my new home. I was almost sent to a girls home because I was told my Mother chose him over me. This I later found out from my Mother was not true. She ended up bailing him out of jail and he lived at our house for a little while longer. I on the other hand had no choice. I was sent away unable to return there even for a visit. I couldn't even get my things from home. My Mother had to bring them to me. It wasn't the best situation for any of us, but that was the way it had to be. I regretted opening my freaking mouth but at the same time I was relieved. I knew that night I would not be tied up or forced to do acts I didn't want to do. I was finally safe. Daddy couldn't hurt me ever again. Months went by and there were court dates, counseling and group therapy for me to face.

The final court date was here. My turn to finally go in front of a judge and tell them all that happened and put him away for good. I was told I would be disowned, no one would ever be with me again and he would die. I feeling so confused, said what everyone had told me I had to say. I lied. I told the mediator that I was lying all to get attention. This wasn't true, but I ended up letting him go so my Mother could have the man she loved and still is with and so my Brother could have his Father. (My Brother was never harmed). That same day we were all released and I was going home with my family. Scared but assured it would never happen again.

I was never more wrong. Before my prom he tried it again. This time I told him with a pair of shearing scissors to his chest. If he ever tried touching me again or anyone else I would KILL him. He stopped instantly to never try anything again. Finally I stood up for myself and had put an end to all of it once and for all. For years I was fine never a problem. Things went the way they should have all along, but there was a problem. I wasn't okay. I was terrified to sleep, to be alone with him, I had nightmares (still do) and the mental pain and abuse then began. He was inside my head still harming me. I couldn't escape.

The mental pain was taking it's toll on me. I started taking sleeping pills, cutting myself, purging even more, exercising all the time and trying to harm myself actually kill myself as quickly as possible without putting a gun to my head. I had taken bottles of sleeping pills and pain killers trying to commit suicide and it never worked. I finally turned Eighteen. My worries were over, I could leave. Not. I had no money to leave with, no place to go and definitely no college. My Brother never believed anything with my Father happened and he walked in on it when I was a child. Oh well. That part of my life is over.

I still have a good relationship with my Mother and we are the best of friends. I was able to forgive her for not knowing what was going on under her nose, loving a man like she did and for staying with him, but I will never forget. We all choose our own paths of how we deal and accept the traumas in our lives, even when no one else understands them. This choice was hers to make and not mine. I love her regardless of her choices as she loves me regardless of mine.

~Sapphire~

Some ways of "coping" with abuse are blocking it all out, knowing it happened but not letting it take a toll on you(for the time being), getting counseling, taking medications or calling a friend as well as writing a journal or poetry. Regardless of which way you "cope" with the abuse you have been put through eventually when you actually have to face your abuse, your attacker or both that is when the true trauma begins. You may start seeing the abuse when you are sleeping, when you are awake, when someone says or does something that reminds you or when someone you love touches you.

These are normal reactions and you should know that until you face your fears dead on and work through the pain, you will not be able to heal. It is very traumatic and so hard to accept I know, but it must be dealt with.

No one can make it better for you, it all has to come from within you to survive. Though the pain will most likely will never go away completely and you will definitely never forget you can be a survivor. With time and strength you can and will heal.

When I think about the pain, my abuse has caused me, all I can do is cry. I relive each memory one by one feeling as terrified as I did at that very moment. I can remember saying "Please Stop!" and "No!" millions of time but it all just continued without hope. I would wait until it was all over only to feel the pain and trauma continue a never ending cycle as the next time began.

Afraid to open the door because someone may know, they will see the bruises and wonder how I could let this happen or won't care anyway or they would have not let it happen in the first place. Threatened with it only being worse next time if I tell anyone what has happened. Going through life living inside a shell afraid to open my heart to anyone. "Don't let the wall down, everyone is the same way" you believe are the words to live by. You can feel yourself breaking into different personalities just to hide the many feelings you hold inside.

One being the strong one able to endure the pain. Another, the one to block it out and not let it harm you mentally. Another, one you label the liar. This is the one who can keep your secrets about the pain and abuse from everyone so it won't be worse next time. Then there is the one who just wants to destroy you and finish you off. Killing yourself seems to be the only answer to end the pain and to never let the abuse happen again.

Cutting yourself to see and feel the abuse flow from your body. You become numb, unable to feel the pain you are causing to yourself at that very moment. All you feel is the abuse and shame leaving your body and the tears flowing from your red swollen eyes. I know from experience how much of a rush this can be. I also know this is not the way to deal with your trauma.

By doing this you are giving the person who caused you harm by abusing you too much power. The more pain the abuse causes you, the more control it has over you. No one deserves to have control over you in this way. Cutting and Self-Injury is not the answer to your trauma. Finding ways to recover and heal, taking back your power and control will make you able to show them how strong you really are. Love yourself enough to make the choice to heal, don't allow anyone to hurt you again in this way. In time though you never will forget, you can regain your self-esteem, self-respect and your mental well being.

Regardless how many victims I hear from on abuse and eating disorders, every story falls into the same category. Horrific and brutal to the well being of us all. We have been through experiences that most cannot begin to imagine. Maybe this is why so many people cannot relate to us when we do try to talk about our problems.

I think that we all feel so lost and have a hard time remembering when we felt happy or "whole" before our disorder. Many of us who have an eating disorder were at one time or another a dancer, cheerleader, model, actress, singer, wrestler, athlete or an abuse survivor of some type of physical or mental abuse.

It is absolutely amazing how these circumstances or activities become so important or are so traumatic depending on the individual, that we are willing to destroy our bodies and devastate our lives. Is all of this really worth being what society believes to be perfect, popular, trendy or acceptable? No it is not.

To look at it from a loved ones point of view is so hard for us to do because we are trapped inside our own destructive cycle with no hope or control. I am going to attempt to give you an example of what someone who loves you goes through when we are going through an eating disorder.

Through my recovery process I have come to care very deeply about others who are suffering from eating disorders. It feels like the more you care or try to help someone you love, the more impossible it is for them to heal. You reach your hand out to catch someone who is falling so quickly that you can only watch them fall to their death slowly unable to help them.

I can now look back and see how much pain this causes to those who love us everyday when we battle Ed. I can hear the crying of my family shrieking through my heart like a dull blade taking my breath away. The devastation and pain that pierces my soul is unbearable knowing I have caused them this broken heart. It is as if they have already lost the person they have been trying to save from a cancer eating them alive. Watching them fail day by day one breath at a time.

    I took care of my Great Aunt for over a year and a half and watched her go from a vibrant, loving and strong willed woman, into a person living inside a shell. She went from feeding, grooming and enjoying herself everyday, to someone who had to eat with a baby dropper and being bathed in bed unable to move or speak. Before she passed on she was an angel waiting for her wings to develop so she could fly home to watch over us.

    I cannot begin to tell you how impossible it was to feel so much love for someone and be unable to ease their pain and suffering. I would pray for God to take away her pain and set her free every day. On the day she passed on, that morning I told her that we all loved her and we knew she loved us. I told her it would be okay, she needed to let go and go to sleep. I said goodbye knowing letting her go was best for her. Of course we all mourned for the loss of her and I still to this day have not truly grieved for the loss of her or my other family members, but this is my way of coping. I knew losing her was the beginning of losing nearly all of the people whom I loved more than I loved myself. Soon after I lost my Uncle to Emphysema, Cancer, and Lung Disease. Another Great Aunt, then my Aunt to Renal Failure, my Grandmother ten days after my Aunt and just recently my last surviving Aunt.

    I can count on one hand, five little fingers those I have left in my family whom I love. All who have desperately tried to help me through my pain. As I write this my eyes are filled with tears dreading feeling the loss of all my loved ones. This is how it feels to our families and friends who love us to watch us die from an eating disorder. They see us dying, rather killing ourselves everyday knowing they cannot save us.

    So the next time your Mother, Father or someone who loves you wants to help you or is begging you to recover, please take any measure necessary to heal. Unlike their being no cure for Cancer, Dementia, Renal Failure or other Diseases. We are the cure for treating Anorexia and Bulimia. We are the antidote to these deadly diseases. Through love, support, faith and inner strength we can overcome our eating disorders and become whole again.

Control

The part of my eating disorder that causes me the hardest struggle in the battle for recovery is Ed controls me. I want to control myself. While I am in recovery, I am in control, Ed can only control what I allow him to control. I need to stand strong, yet I not only miss but crave the ability to have someone else especially Ed make the hard decisions for me.

I am not happy about recovery in a sense because I am setting free all that kept me "strong" in my eyes. I am however proud of myself for finally truly wanting to heal. I am slowly learning how to use control to make my life the way I want it to be. I may never love myself or like the way I look completely, but I am who I am and no one can take this away from me. I am proud of the person I am becoming and in time it will only get better.

Some believe that you are in control of your own destiny, I beg to differ. I know for the "normal" people out there this may be true, but for sufferers of Abuse or Eating Disorders and Depression this is not the case. We have several different reasons we cannot control ourselves in the same manner as others. It may be that we hear a voice inside our heads telling us to do something different from what we would like to do, it could be that our peers are showing us different paths that may seem fun or cool, it could even be that from our loved ones we are shown the wrong ways of handling situations or dealing and facing our fears and things that happen to us.

I wish that control was something that I could have had for the last twenty-four years but the simple truth is, I had none. Zero, zilch, nada. The more I wanted it the less I had and the more I found I had no clue on how to gain it.

We find ways to make excuses of why we cannot stop our binging, purging or restricting. Why when we know at some point we must stop or we will die, we don't quit? We make excuses for everything we feel is too difficult to do or stop doing even though we know it has to be done. Ed gives us the excuses to say and we allow him to control us. We must break this chain and the ties that hold him to us. I know it is not easy, it is very hard to do, but we can make him fade until he one day disappears.

If Ed tells you to lie, force yourself to tell the truth. If Ed tells you to binge, purge, restrict whatever, put it in your mind that you refuse to listen. He can only control you if you give him that power. Take away the power and he has nothing to use against you. Just like when you were young and your parents would tell you "If your friends jumped off a bridge, does that mean you have to?" Does Ed make this harder for us? Yes. But it is the same scenario. He can say whatever he wants to you, but you know right form wrong. So don't listen to him and don't do as he commands you. When we are active in our Eating Disorder, we are slaves to Ed.

How can one voice be so powerful that it can reach millions of us every day? You may think that because I am in recovery, I have forgotten how hard all of this really is. The truth is it gets even harder with recovery. You are constantly looking over your shoulder trying to see if he is back. Any day Ed could walk back in your life. As soon as you let your guard down and you believe you are okay, this is when Ed abuses you the worst. You have no choice but to fight back and win. So believe me when I say I understand, relate and truly know how hard it is to recover. Just like a drug or alcohol addict, once you are in an eating disorder, you are a victim and addict forever.

You will always have to heal one day at a time for the rest of your life. There are several times a day I want to go back to my old habits, believe me it is easier to let someone else have this control. But I cannot and will not do it. I have worked too hard and have gained too much by being the one in charge and I will not let this go. I pray everyday that God will give me the strength to fight Ed and not let him back into my life again.

Guilt

There is so much guilt involved with an Eating Disorder, Abuse and Self-Injury. It puts you in a lonely state of mind causing depression. Nothing you do seems to be right, nothing you say can make the ones you love believe you will stop your behavior, and the shame you feel takes over your everyday lives.

First let's start out with being unable to do the right thing. You feel as if no matter what choice you make it will be the wrong one. For example, Ed tells you to have dinner and it will be okay, you have earned the ability to eat today. False. Ed is really telling you that you are fat, weak, you have no willpower and if you do eat dinner you had better purge it immediately. So if and when you finally eat this is what you obsess over knowing it means pain and the gross taste of regurgitated food being your dessert. Not to mention you have to hide from everyone to purge or they will know what you are doing. Does this sound familiar to you? I know it does to me because this is what I go through all the time with Ed. The other option being starve yourself, Ed tells you not to eat dinner because you haven't suffered enough to deserve to eat dinner because you haven't lost enough weight yet, you're still fat and disgusting looking and until you lose enough weight this is the way it is going to be.

Then there is the Self-Injury and depression side of this. You need to feel the release of the food, abuse or whatever has sent you to this state of being. Your guilty because you did or did not listen to Ed when you were suppose to, the problems you are going through are getting the best of you or the abuse happened and you feel it was your fault. False again. You never asked to be abused or raped, hell you never want to imagine those things ever happening and Ed certainly is not the one who is right by telling you if you deserve to eat or not. Who the hell is he anyway. You should be the one that controls these things not Ed.

You know if and when you are hungry so eat damn it! (famous line of my Fiancé) So by cutting or harming yourself you aren't releasing the abuse, problems or food because once you do this and you are satisfied for that moment, it will make you feel no better because the same problems will be there again next time for you to start this vicious cycle all over again. Whether it be a few minutes, hours, days or weeks the urge will come back and you are the one who will have to choose what to do. Don't let Ed. He is always going to be the wrong choice. You have once again accomplished nothing. All you have done now is made more wounds that have to heal and possibly someone you love seeing them. Here is where some of the depression comes in now. What if someone does see them, what will they think? Will they think I am crazy? Will they try and put me away? Will they care at all?

The fear of being committed is there and so is the fear of no one giving a damn. Finally you may wonder why you are doing this to yourself and why you are hurting the ones that you care about in this way. There is no right answer but to end the self harm and to try and find other outlets for your pain. I am not telling you what to do here, I am only telling you that I know from experience how this all is because I was cutting for years on end until I finally got help and realized the problems don't end. Cutting or self harm only increases them and makes your life a living hell. So please stop harming yourselves. It is not worth all the pain you cause to yourself and those around you who love you.

Next is nothing you says is ever right. There are only so many times you can tell yourself and others nothing happened or it was my fault this is happening or happened to me. One thing to always remember is you never asked to be abused or raped. You are never to blame and the pain you endured during the abuse was enough pain. You don't need to add to it by injuring yourself. It won't make the pain end and it won't make the abuse fade away. It only turns into self abuse and honestly you have a choice in that and it can be prevented. So Don't Do It!

Ed will tell you things to say like I am not hungry or I have already eating. Bullshit. Enough is Enough! You didn't eat and you are beyond hungry, you are starving and what is worse your body is begging to be fed. Your organs need food to survive or you will die. Regardless of what you might believe, I myself have to especially feed the one and only kidney I have. I couldn't be given another one later on down the line if this one fails because my body would most likely reject it. So yes guilty or not, fat or weak I must eat. There are so many foods out there you can eat and not gain weight by just simply eating. You just have to be sensible and eat. The one thing that happens if you keep starving yourself is by the time you actually allow yourself to eat you binge and eat everything you can till you are sick because your body is craving so much. Then you purge and the cycle starts all over again.

There are millions of people dying from starvation every year and trust me they aren't choosing to starve. There is just no food for them to eat, yet we choose to starve ourselves or purge the food that could be fed to these hungry babies, children, adolescents, adults and elderly. This is a good reason to feel guilty because you are doing something wrong. We all are. I take my blame for this too. What if just the amounts we have purged could save a person's life, are we then inhumane for being so selfish? Hell yes we are. I am ashamed of myself when I think about it like that. Just what I purged could save someone's life if they were to eat it. Imagine how many lives we could save. This is truly a crime.

Finally feeling shame. In the last paragraph I explained shame when it comes to how badly Ed can affect us. The shame from abuse or rape cannot be reversed. Reason being is shame comes along with rape or abuse for no good reason other than to make us feel worse. The difference is we can take control of Ed and Self-Injury because it begins and ends with us. Abuse or rape is not a choice we made happen. I am not saying we choose to have an Eating Disorder, what I am saying is we choose to let it continue and not heal. If we want it to end then we can make it happen and recover. Life is filled with difficult choices and to end a relationship with Ed or deciding to stop purging, restricting, binging, cutting, burning or to stop all destructive behavior is a choice and we need to make the choice now.

Autumn Christ

Emptiness

The hardest part of my eating disorder has been the emptiness and the loneliness inside my soul. I still feel the pain eating me alive every day. So many days I have just wanted to go to sleep and never wake up. Those days still happen all the time. I still don't know which hurts me more, the memories of my abuse from my ex-boyfriend or knowing I have caused myself this pain.

I think not being able to have children causes me to feel so empty inside. This is the worst thing in my life. That pain is unbearable and heartbreaking. I would give my life to have children even one at this point (I wanted twelve), but there has just been too much damage done to my body. If I were rich, the first thing I would do would be to find a way to have children and at the same time adopt several other children who are in need of a good home and a loving family.

I know I am not now nor ever will be rich but I will find a way hopefully by the year 2005 to adopt at least one baby. Girl or boy it doesn't matter, as long as he or she is healthy. I will do everything in my power to protect them and give them all I can with unconditional love and affection. I will never have my child go through the things in my life I have gone through and I will always assure my child that I love them just the way they are, for who they are and not because of how society should make them feel they have to become.

I can only ask that this book offers something to our parents which can teach them more on how to relate to us and for those parents who feel we need to be as society says we do, I would like to tell them to stop judging us because I know they don't want or like to be judged themselves. Please remember we are human beings not machines and if you want perfection, know the price is too high to pay.

Insomnia

When you are suffering, feeling guilty are relapsing whatever the case may be you are unable to sleep. This is what they call insomnia. Something your mind does to you when you have too much or major stress on your mind. Regardless of what causes the insomnia it is just as hard on you as the weight you have on your shoulders already. There are medications that you can take from anti-depressants, anti-anxiety and sleeping pills to ease this symptom, but the only way to cure the insomnia is to eventually figure out what is making it impossible for you to sleep and to face your trauma and eating disorder head on so you can work towards a healthy recovery.

Continuing the purging rituals, binging or the self harm will only make you feel and look worse everyday and eventually kill you. We always say this will never to happen to us, we are immortal because we don't need to eat, feel, sleep or love. These are the things that show weakness and mortality. It takes major strength to do what we do on a daily basis. All I can say is none of us are immortal and we will die eventually, but why throw away the miracle of life and make ourselves suffer so much when we are going to be taken when God is ready for us to be with him again. Otherwise we will burn in hell from the suicide we cause ourselves.

Healing is the hardest thing to do for ourselves, but it must be done in order for us to see just how precious life really is. Nothing can beat us if we don't allow ourselves to give in. Though we have had trauma that we feel should have killed us by now, we are still here unlike those who have been so unfortunate to have lost their lives from their abuse, eating disorder, self-injury and suicidal acts.

Think about it like this, the abuse we suffer from may have been harder than anything to imagine, but we have survived because we are still here. The self-mutilation we cause ourselves is scarring and painful yet we are alive to have a second chance at healing. Though we may be starving ourselves now or we are overeating and purging till we feel like we are dying from the pain. All of this passes and we have another opportunity to say no, I am better than this and I can recover.

Everyday I continue to write this book, I see more and more how dumb yet sick I really am and have been for twenty-four years. At the same time I am seeing how precious life is because I am still here and I am choosing recovery. I have been given the opportunity to help you see how important it is to heal. My goal on this earth and in my life is to save as many lives possible for as long as I am here. I still suffer from insomnia, but the difference is I am having positive stress and so many good things on my mind to achieve I cannot sleep.

So you see our worst struggles have been given to us so we can become stronger, live a better life and find our place here on earth to do all the things we have never imagined possible for us to do before. The next time you cannot sleep, try and figure out a way you can help someone else because there are millions of way to do so and put one thing in your life or into yourself that is positive and good into your mind and sleep well. This can be done but you have to want it bad enough.

Nightmares

Have you ever noticed the bigger your relapse, when you are most active in you eating disorder, or self-injury the more nightmares occur when you sleep. the dreams can be about anything literally even some things that you have nothing to do with. Sometimes they are right on target. They will be about many things regarding your eating disorder. Foods you do and do not allow yourself to indulge in. They could be about being so sick you can feel yourself leaving your body. Death is another big nightmare, only this one seems to be a relief for us. These are only examples and as we go through the next few pages you will see the different ways they affect us and the pain they cause as well as some relief.

There are dreams about your abuse. Where, when, how it happened and who was involved. The worst one is when you face your attacker all over again and you are stuck in the fear unable to move, breathe, fight back or wake up. These are the dreams that make you feel you need a release, so you end up harming yourself or feeling suicidal. Easier said than done I know, but you have to keep calm, know it is a nightmare and nothing can hurt you anymore. You will be okay because you are able to wake up and look around seeing familiar things, faces, and know you are safe again. The hardest thing which makes the trauma so bad is if you personally know the attacker and one time or another you have to face them on a regular basis. This will be a definite trigger for you and be the main cause of your nightmares and eating disorder or self-injury.

Sometimes when you suffer from self-injury you face this trauma in your dreams. You see the different ways of cutting, burning or the several objects you can use to cause harm to yourself. This is when you need to wake yourself up and breathe deeply so you can get your bearings and not harm yourself. It takes so much strength to overcome self-injury but you can do it. You have to promise yourself not others when you want to stop because above all you cannot allow yourself to be disappointed. The same goes with your eating disorder, do not disappoint yourself. I am not saying that other people you love don't count or it is unimportant to keep your promises to them as well, what I am saying is you have to put yourself first in your recovery regardless of what that recovery is.

Your eating disorder nightmares are just as difficult as the previous ones because you run the risk of falling deeper into the cycle of your eating disorder when you have nightmares. The silliest dream of food chasing you could scare you when you have an eating disorder. I know for me I just recently had a nightmare that Ed was telling me I should not eat in my dream and if I did he would cause my mouth to bleed. I ignored Ed, but woke up from my nightmare with a bloody mouth. I probably bit my tongue or cheek, something but the dream was so real to me and not something I want to deal with again. Eating disorders cause your mind to believe in things that are not really true, just like dreams you are unable to understand and scare you.

So when you have nightmares please know they aren't real, they are your mind finding ways to heal and face your disease and pain. Do not allow them to take over your life. Whether it is Ed, your abuser or you being your own enemy with self-injury. Become your own best friend, put yourself on a pedestal and know as well as believe you deserve recovery and you are worth saving. If you don't believe in yourself, no one else truly can. Our goal is recovery and believing in ourselves is half the battle along with good self-esteem. Please start believing in yourself now one day at a time and become the person you have always wanted to be in life.

Strength

Everyday we fight an endless battle within ourselves and everyday we have a choice to win or lose. Sometimes it is easier to pretend our strength comes from letting Ed decide for us. Other days it is a great accomplishment to win against Ed. I have had more bad rather than good days in my struggles with Ed. This tells me that Ed can be overcome, because even one good day means recovery is in fact attainable.

I have found that if I just talk back to Ed, I can find the strength to win against him. He is so powerful and overwhelming that it is easier to give in, but we just cannot stand back and give a voice this much strength. It is bad enough when we give those around us the power to choose what is best for us.

Half the time we get mad at our parents or other loved ones if they tell us what to do or give us a curfew, so why don't we fight or argue with Ed when he tells us what to do? Because he comes from trauma or upset that is caused by our relationships or experiences from those we love and protects us we believe.

Sometimes things are said to us that people don't believe could ever hurt us either in a joking or serious manner. The truth is words usually do hurt us more than physical pain. Here is an example. If our parent spanks or disciplines us by taking something tangible we either get over the anger quickly from being hit or find something else to use to occupy our time.

But if we are told that we must stop what we are doing at a certain time or say to us we are stupid, worthless or call us other derogatory names, we are more likely to feel the anger or hurt more and for a longer period of time.

I remember when I was a child feeling so weak and defenseless because I would be called names by other children, some so called friends and certain family members. Most of the time the words from family or friends were out of fun when we would pick with each other to pass time. But someone like myself who has the history I do, it would make me feel like they were serious.

Examples are names like stupid, dumb ass, ugly, fat, hey kool-aid, chubby, heavy set or pain in the ass. These words became triggers for me. I would and still feel like I am just a burden, I weigh too much or I am not pretty enough to fit in or be accepted. I keep these feelings inside because I am afraid to let people know they hurt me.

We all know kids are cruel, but during my childhood they seemed down right mean. Because I had kidney problems, I would have to often skip playing at recess or lunch in school because if I did I would wet myself. It couldn't be helped. I had no control of my bladder. So the kids called me names like ms. pee body, piss pants and betsy wetsy. These names followed me from kindergarten to my tenth grade year in high school. I changed schools when we moved to another city about an hour away where no one knew me and I no longer was called those names.

I don't remember having boys liking me or girls wanting me to come to slumber parties because they were afraid I would pee at their house and ruin their parties. I found my best friend to be Ed throughout the years.

I found myself acting like a shy and timid little girl afraid to speak my mind and have the strength to stand up for myself. I would later on get into physical fights because the hostility and anger would get the best of me from being treated this way. So I would retaliate. Our strength develops over time when we have reached our limit with the way we are talked to or treated. We just come to the point that enough is enough and if we don't let it all out, it will eat us alive or turns into a disorder like Ed.

Once Ed or a personality disorder develops it is too late. The monster is created and before you know it our strength is transferred to someone or something else. Ed has been my strength and guide for so long, I don't know who I am or who I can be without him. These past four months, I have been searching to find the real me and who I am without Ed. Writing this book about my disorder has helped me so much, yet I have so far to go.

I want to one day be able to have all my strength back that I have given away to my abuse, Ed and those who hurt me. I want to turn it all into a positive driving force and make my life better. I know I want to help others and my goal is to become strong enough to fight Ed for life. I want to finally say I won and Ed cannot hurt me anymore. I am on that path now, I just keep praying that I can succeed. One day at a time is the best and only way I can do it, good or bad.

Autumn Christ

Loving Yourself

We all want to find love and be loved by those closest to us. The reality is we don't know how to love ourselves. The old saying "you can't love someone else unless you love yourself" or "how can someone else love you if you don't love yourself" are such true statements. We may have those in our family, friendship circle and/or even our significant others loving us, but imagine how much better that love could be if we could share in that love ourselves.

We wouldn't be harming ourselves in one way, shape or form anymore. We would be able to smile, laugh, be happy for once, hold our heads up high when we walk and even be secure in ourselves knowing we are as beautiful inside as others see us on the outside. We would also see us in the eyes of another and find the beauty they see in us. This would bring me the happiest and most loved feeling in the world. Just think how nice it would be to admire ourselves.

There are many different ways to build ones self-esteem and self-image. The first one which I always thought to be boring and dumb was to look in the mirror and say "I am beautiful" everyday three times a day. Believe it or not after doing this long enough it does work. I say I am beautiful and the self-image I see slowly begins to change. At first it may be embarrassing just like your first day at a class for yoga, meditation or anything new would be. But once you open your mind, focus your energy on yourself and find who you are, you can be proud of yourself for trying to begin to heal. Only then you can find that it does help you and works quite amazingly.

We always say things like if I could look like this person or that person I would be happy, we may even say how if we had the life of our favorite celebrity we would be happy. The truth is we may never see this happen in our lives because the likelihood is so minimal that we just say we can never be happy and set ourselves up to fail. This is what causes us to go into a depression, crying, harming ourselves in one way or another and begin avoiding those we love and who love us. FOR WHAT? To face the simple reality that we will still must live, we must work, go to school, look as we do and be who we are.

So what have we accomplished by making these statements… NOTHING! We are human beings not machines or robots that can be programmed to be perfect and never make mistakes. The most beautiful, rich and talented people in the world make mistakes, have flaws they hate about themselves or are some of the most unhappy people in the world.

Ask yourself this question:

If you could have the most loving family in the world and be poor, or have all the money in the world to buy anything and everything you could want yet have no love in your life from anyone…which would you choose?

Eating Disorders, Depressive Disorders, Self-Injury and daily life are the same as this question. If we kill ourselves by doing whatever it takes to be thin, beautiful or loved, we lose. But if we love ourselves first and share that love with others we are the richest of all. Money can always be made, materialistic things can always be attained, but self-esteem and self-love are the two things that we all must really look for and find to achieve our goals.

I say this because I have been there and still am in many ways, but I also have the most precious gift in the world that money, fame, looks and size can never bring me. I have love for others and unconditional love from others by loving myself first.

Another exercise I have used to help me is this book. I am not saying to heal you must write a book. What I am saying is this book began because

I wanted to help others and in turn help myself. So I began writing in a journal, as if my problems were a friends and I would give that friend advice and the help they needed to feel better about themselves and be a better person. From then on, I found myself writing a book on self-help which is really someone pointing you in the right direction you yourself already knew you needed to go. I am not saying I am happy others are suffering, because that is the furthest from the truth. But it does help us to know we are not alone in our struggles against Ed.

Funny isn't it how someone who can relate to your situations can help you see things in a different light. I know it has helped me and I am so thankful for there being others out there who have done what I have done and have recovered or are in recovery now. Knowing I am not alone really helps. At the same time I wish none of us ever had to go through this pain.

Autumn Christ

Relationships

Relationships are so different to have when you suffer from an eating disorder. Trust and respect are the main factors in a relationship and they both must start with love before they can blossom. The next few pages of this book will talk about the factors that lead to a healthy and happy relationship from my point of view. This is what works for me and I believe is the basis for anyone in search of a good foundation for a relationship. No matter who it is with.

First there is respect, you must give respect as well as receive respect. This is earned to an extent, but expected and should always be demanded upon in a relationship. Respect can be something as small as considering your loved ones feelings first, to compromising when you disagree on something and coming to a strong solution to fix the problem you are having. If you cannot respect yourself, it will be much harder to receive respect from someone else. The reason for this is you won't know what you are supposed to have from someone else.

In abuse cases, survivors accept what they have rather than what they want most of the time because we don't know what true respect and love is since it was violated so harshly. We don't know what respect should be about because we haven't had it before. Abuse or rape can violate more than just your mind and body it can violate your relationships for the future and diminish your self-deserving qualities. I know from experience that once you are abused, you feel as though what you have is the best you could ever have. This is not true. You deserve to have someone think of you first in their lives. You should never be second place to anyone. First and foremost you must be first in your life. Never worry about another person more than you do yourself or you take the risk of not knowing who you are as a person but who you are with that person.

Find yourself first and be strong in who you are before you consider being in a relationship because if not, you run the risk of never having respect, loyalty or true love from someone else. You must love yourself above anyone else first. I never believed in this until I chose to be alone and find out who I really was and what I honestly deserved and wanted for myself. I then found someone who gives me exactly what I was looking for. Self-love is most important in any relationship beyond trust, respect, loyalty or love.

Trust is the next factor. It is earned from both people and never demanded. You have to deserve to be trusted by being faithful and honest and show your loyalty to the person you are in the relationship with through your love. People believe that you should just go ahead and trust another person, but I believe that if someone wants you to trust them they must show you what trust is by giving it to you as well. No one in a relationship can guarantee even the smallest of promises like the sun will shine tomorrow, because if it doesn't then you are considered a liar. You have no control about the sun shining, but you do have control over what you do as a person.

If you want to be trusted in a relationship, then you must also give trust as well as earn it by showing your honesty and loyalty. Anyone can say oh I trust you or I can be trusted I promise. Well if you know in your heart that you cannot keep that promise then why make it? If you cannot trust yourself how can anyone else trust you and if you don't have trust in a relationship no matter how much love is there you really have no relationship at all. I have made empty promises with my eating disorder so many times and have lost some of the trust that I once had, but I have spent everyday promising myself I would earn that trust back no matter what. Why? Because I love the people that I have hurt by breaking their trust and I am truly sorry for that.

They know that I was out of control with my eating disorder and that I was not acting like myself by hiding diet pills, laxatives, ipecac, restricting, purging and over exercising. I am giving no excuse for this because I did it to myself. Now that I am stronger in my recovery I see the harm it did and everyday I am trying harder to gain that trust I lost. I believe that I have earned a lot of it back, because everyone sees just how important I have become to myself as well as how important they are to me. My recovery now is the most important thing to me and it must stay that way until I am completely in control and my recovery is complete.

I am choosing to put myself first in my life through independence, self-love, trust and respect. It may sound funny being said this way but it is the way it must be for me and no one is going to take this away from me. I will not ruin what I have worked so hard to achieve. That is trusting, respecting and showing loyalty and self-love to myself and I know I am a better person for doing this. Ed is gone and he is not returning.

Autumn Christ

Faith

When we have an eating disorder it is hard to tell if and when we are ever really hungry or just craving wanting to binge. The best way to change this horrible pattern is to try eating several small meals a day. Even if it means every two or three hours we have a small snack. Our bodies are going to slowly go through the re-feeding process and our metabolism will have to slowly start working again. I know that you are thinking your stomach will hurt or you will have to purge immediately, but you don't have to.

I am speaking from experience not as an outsider. Your stomach will feel full, cramp up and the purging sensation will be there, but you must fight it. You can make it through the pain and only you can control the gag reflex to keep from purging. It does take a long time and will not happen overnight, but the pain will eventually ease. There is only one person who can make you recover and that is you.

Your doctor can help ease this process for you as well through medications, support and even possible hospitalization, but you must do what it takes to heal. Together you, your doctor and your family can Overcome Your ED. Faith, religion or believing in someone or something with a higher power will help you also. When we are lost and alone feeling empty inside it is hard to believe in anything or anyone. There is a higher being who can help you, all you need to do is open your mind and your heart and have the desire to once again be whole. I know in the beginning of my eating disorder I felt lost and alone all I could do was cry. I would beg for this pain to end. I would repeatedly say "Please God take this pain away, make it stop!"

Finally one day I had no choice but to put all my faith, trust and belief in him and pray the pain would ease. I had hit rock bottom and more than once. I just never knew it. I finally felt some of the pain ease and feel the want to recover. When your doctor's are calling you a walking corpse and you are hospitalized wearing a heart monitor and tubes in your veins and down your throat, believe me you have hit rock bottom. Just like an alcoholic or drug addict. Until you hit the bottom there is no coming up. I went from having ten to twenty seizures a day, unable to drive or work for three years to having the strength to write this book for you. I am now able to work a part-time job, wake up with a purpose, feel good about myself and have people around me who love me for me daily. Talk about a turn around. From death to life in a battle that has taken me twenty-four years too long to win.

I will be praying everyday for all of you to find whatever being or power it is for you to believe in to recover and gain some strength to fight your own battles and win the wars. I would like everyone to be able to heal and have a better life than you have now.

If your family won't support you then find a support group, a good friend to spend time with or a help line number to call when you feel a relapse or twinge of Ed coming on. There is support there if you need it, but you have to ask for help in order to receive it. Please know that your families do care and love you, they sometimes just do not know how to show it. Try to see through what they are saying or doing and find what it is they are trying to achieve for you.

I promise you if they truly love you and want to help they will listen and learn more about your disorder so they can better understand what you are going through. Take the time to ask them for the help you so dearly need. They want to help, they just don't know how to reach you. So show them the way of how to help and don't give up on them. They will not give up on you regardless of what they say they love you deep within their souls. They may tell you to just stop it now, but you know if it were that easy none of us would have eating disorders. Explain this to them and make them see that you feel so alone in this battle and you need to receive help.

Hospitalization I promise you is not the worst thing in the world, dying before you know who or what you can become is the worst thing in the world that could happen to you.

Autumn Christ

Life's Little Curves

Sometimes life throws you a curve and how you deal with it will determine the outcome. This is the same with your eating disorder. We don't choose to have one but here we are right in the middle of it. Now the question is what are we going to do with it? Are we going to let Ed take over our lives like he has done so many times before, or are we going to tell him to leave. Just like someone you are in a relationship with and no longer want to be a part of. The tie must be broken. The hard part isn't saying good bye, the hard part is refusing to let them back in. I found getting rid of my ex-boyfriend to be the easiest and best thing to do with my life. With Ed it has truly been a challenge.

The reason being is for twenty-four years he has been my protector, my guide and my strength when I have been weak, or so I thought. Reality is he was just as bad for me as my ex was. I am glad that I am now rid of both of them and able to build a new life with a man I am truly in love with and most importantly, I love myself enough to know what and who is best for me. I not only feel much better physically, but mentally I am in the best frame of mind in my life. I can think clearly, focus on important issues that need my attention and I can hold my head high knowing I am important and deserve to be well. I am beginning to love my life and myself more and more everyday. The best feeling in the world is to be able to love yourself and be proud of who you are.

I don't want to backslide ever again and I will do my best not to. When Ed comes back and I know he will try very hard to do so, I will once again tell him he is not welcome and he must leave now. I am better off without him. I love my life just as it is right now and plan on keeping it this way only to get better from here on out. You can do the same just take the first step and see how wonderful life can be for you. Others around you will be as proud of you as you are of yourself.

Past Vs. Future

You cannot dictate your past, but you can make your future better than you ever imagined possible. Through your pain and trauma, you are still here and able to heal if your soul desires. Though I cannot change my past or forget what has happened to me, I can make my present self see a more positive side and bright new future. I have to accept and admit to the damage I have done to myself not only what others have done to me in order for me to fully heal.

I ultimately decided to cause pain to myself through my eating disorder by allowing Ed to control me. The abuse I have suffered in the past has led me on a path for destruction, but my eating disorder started way before the abuse ever did. I have been abusing myself longer than anyone has. My ex-boyfriend may have caused trauma for ten years to my self-esteem, body and mind. I am the true cause of allowing the abuse to happen it seems. I started the ugly process at nine years old with taking laxatives, harming myself, restricting and purging and over exercising. I have put my body in this state and have caused my past to dictate my future.

Now I must make this turn around and find myself and allow no one to interfere with my healing and well being. Your past can make you feel like there is no hope whatsoever left in life, but this isn't true. You can make your past strengthen you to have a more positive and lively future.

Autumn Christ

Journal Entries

This chapter consists of journal entries from myself as well as others who have chosen to share their experiences with you. Some of these entries can be hard to read and others you may be able to relate to very well. The reason this part of the book was so important to me was to show you that you are not alone and we all struggle with many of the same issues everyday.

Please realize that this was a voluntary process and please don't judge any of us for what you are about to read, but learn from our mistakes and situations. Try to find a way to heal with us and make your life better one day at a time. Please don't feel that these are ways to help you in harming yourself, are "new ways" to lose weight, continue your destruction or conceal your efforts. Eventually it all comes to an ugly head and will destroy you and your loved ones without notice or fail.

Autumn Christ

Autumn's Journal Entries

Dear Journal,

At thirty-two years old I am still petrified of my past. I cannot seem to shake it no matter how hard I try. I have made mistakes myself I know, but to even dream that the nightmare would continue for so long is unbearable. I hate myself for allowing him to hurt me. I should have killed the bastard. The pain is never ending and the sad yet undeniable truth is that I have done everything I could to erase it and it will never be okay.

I am still that little child inside trying to break free from the abuse that continues to haunt me and will forever. I am so scared. I will never be okay and I will only be free once I am no longer living. I need to be alone and I need to hide from my fears forever. There is no point in trying to have a relationship when so many I have had in my life have been based on pain and fear. I am terrified to live another day. I need severe help and I know that if I get it, I will lose everything and everyone I have worked so hard at having in my life. I feel now my life will be over and I will cease to exist. I don't want to hurt those who love me, I only want to disappear as if I have never existed.

I have prayed over and over again for miracles, knowing the miracle is how long I have been able to fight all this penned up anger and fear. It is on the verge of coming out now and the only question is can I survive the pain I am about to be facing and will the ones I love be there when it is over, if it can every truly be over? Leaving is the right choice staying is devastation and destruction for all.

~Autumn~

Dear Journal,

A day with the family is a scary day for me because it means I have to eat, swim and put on a bathing suit in front of other people. The rest of the day will be great as we sit around talking about how we are all doing, laughing and smiling and just having a good time. I have been in a suit around the same people I am with now (my family) over a dozen times and it is getting easier with them every time. Reason being is because they don't judge me, make fun of me or even care what I look like when I swim in my suit or what I eat. In fact eating is encouraged and demanded upon.

They all love me for who I am and unconditionally support me in everything I do. I love to spend time with each and every one of them knowing I may be scared inside at the beginning, but it will be okay. I am loved and no one cares what I look like, they just care about me. Ed is talking to me now telling me "how dare you eat what you are eating and who do you think you are strutting around in a suit". "You should be ashamed of yourself now go purge and change back into your regular clothes". But I don't. I hold in the food and I take a deep breath and enjoy the rest of my day.

I have to be normal. There is no longer a choice anymore in choosing this. I want to live! I deserve to live, eat and dress how I want to enjoy myself and feel proud that I am this strong in my recovery. So I tell Ed to "take a hike damn it." I am going to be happy and he is not in control of me anymore. I refuse to let him be. It feels so good to say this and know that I am around a group of people I love and who respect me for me. I am relaxed and secure in who I am and how I look for today anyway. I thank my family for being who they are and for being so good to me. I love you all dearly.

~Autumn~

Dear Journal,

I am going to be facing a tough decision very soon and that decision is whether or not to have a full hysterectomy to relieve the pain I am constantly in because of my Endometriosis. They have tried everything including surgery to ease the scarring and the pain, but nothing is helping. I know this also means I will never be able to have children biologically, but with the supportive man I have standing beside me through it all I know I will be okay.

I think about my Aunt now knowing her and I always had very similar medical problems and I am again following in her footsteps with this and I am so afraid. Yes, I admit it, I am terrified. How do I stop the similarities from continuing in our health conditions? Please God help me make this pain end.

~Autumn~

Dear Journal,

I want to stop cutting but I don't know how anymore. I have been doing it for so long and it feels too good when I feel the release of all my pain fading away. The bad part is when I am done I have to wear something that will cover my scars so no one knows about my private life. It is all that keeps me sane if you can call this sanity. It is my freedom from my pain, I am able to escape my fears and anger by letting it flow from my veins freely.

I don't know which pain is worse, the cutting and hiding or the trauma I have been through and the eating disorder that binds me to lie and deceive everyone. To accept less than perfection is unacceptable when you have an eating disorder. I must find a way to stop cutting because I know it is getting worse everyday and this isn't the way I want to live my life. Please help me!

~Autumn~

Autumn Christ

Poetry

These next pages are filled with poetry from several people who have gone through or are still fighting against Anorexia, Bulimia, Depressive Disorders, self-Injury, Survivors of Abuse and daily life where we all find our own struggles. I wanted to share this poetry with all of you so that you can see all the ways we fight within ourselves to heal or to be perfect, when perfection is unattainable.

We simply are who we are and we have no choice in our shapes, sizes, color, height, weight or family ties. The best we can do is be who we want to be as a person and perfect our minds and souls. Just because society wants us to look a certain way doesn't mean they are right. In reality, if we look at society they show that they are even more screwed up than we are.

Voices In My Head

There are voices in my head telling me to cut myself and make me bleed,
the release of blood is the pain relieved.
I say no more someone will know,
My blood stained sheets and clothes will tell them so.
The cuts and scars are everywhere I look,
Take out paper and a pen you could write a book.
On how to keep from listening to them,
You must keep the blade away from your skin.
You want to stop cutting, but how else can the pain escape?
The voices tell me to cut just one more day.
The pain will continue to build like the pressure in a can of paint,
Now hurry and cut yourself before it is too late.
You know you want the pain to end,
That sharp silver blade is your only friend.
Feel the release of all your pain,
Now cut yourself and let the release begin.

~Anonymous~

What Ed Means to Me

Senseless and demeaning is what having an eating disorder means to me,
Controlling and demanding, Ed is my enemy.
Ashamed and alone is how I feel everyday,
Praying to God he will take my pain and agony away.
Afraid of not listening to the voices inside my head,
Knowing I must stop this insanity before they find me dead.
I have planned my funeral so many times before,
Feeling myself knocking on heaven's door.
What will make this horrific cycle end finally?
Will I die regretting my life and burn in hell for eternity?

Written By: Autumn

Hiding In Plain Sight

Can you see my brightness waning?
Dull eyes no longer reflect my light.
Nothing more than a mere shadow.
I'm hiding in plain sight.

Tortured thoughts consume my waking,
These battles have become my plight.
Inner strength is slowly fading,
I'm hiding in plain sight.

Words have long since lost their meaning,
Though I try with all my might.
Wasted body, criss-cross scars,
I'm hiding in plain sight.

Can you look beyond to find me
Help me win this bitter fight?
I might be standing right next to you,
I'm hiding in plain sight.

Written By: Rosy

    This poem was inspired by the title of this book "Hiding in Plain Sight" and was written by someone whom I have had the pleasure of meeting through my website. Rosy is a beautiful person who tries everyday to recover from SI and I pray that this book will help her to recover.

    I wish you the best Rosy and God Bless You.

    ~Autumn~

What's Going On?

Ashamed of my
Biggest burden
Called to some a simple
Diet, but to me a destroyer
Erasing all my personality.
Forcing me to surrender and
Give in.
Hopelessly trying to grasp onto the
Ideal and unattainable image.
Just to stumble and fall and slowly
Kill the beauty and inside,
Life I once had.
My thoughts flutter from
Not wanting it to be
Over, but
Prayers to get through
Quietly without many unwanted detours and
Right into a recovery.
Sliding slowly
Toward the Process of
Utilizing my inner
Voice and vision of the
Wisdom in acceptance.
Xcitement in
Yearning for reaching out to the final
Zenith.

Written By: Megan

    This poem was written by Megan, a patient in the Partial Hospitalization Program in Hershey. I have been honored to meet you and I am proud of you in your recovery. Keep up the great strength in your battle over ED and

Autumn Christ

never let him take over your life again. You are a beautiful young woman and have so much to give and so much in life to live for. God Bless You.

~Autumn~

What's Going On?

Angry about
Being in the state I am.
Constantly worrying.
Diving into an unknown world.
Everyone encouraging me.
Friends are somewhat there.
Going in circles throughout the day.
Here, there and everywhere.
I want this disorder to leave me alone,
Just fade away.
Koming here has made all the difference.
Laughter, release and friendship.
Many feel the exact same way I do.
Nothing should be holding us back.
Obsessing maybe sets us back.
Prying and pestering
Questions are left unanswered in our busy minds.
Reaching out to others for answers can be difficult.
So many life long relationships grow doing this.
The days come and go as always,
Unbelievably fast.
Vital life lessons are always learned,
Whether we want to or not.
Xing out my problems won't make them fade away.
Y can't it be easy?
Zooms in and out of my mind.

Written By: Emily

This poem was written by Emily, a member of the Partial Hospitalization group in Hershey. I have been inspired by your will to recover. I am proud

Autumn Christ

of you and I wish you the best in your recovery. You are very gifted and your talents will help you reach your goals. God Bless You.

~Autumn~

What's Going On?

Amazingly I have survived
Being the victim of
Control,
Dedicating my life to Ed and wanting to now end my eating disorder so I may feel whole.
Fearing the chance of a relapse, while
Going through the struggle of
Hearing his voice
In my head.
Just yesterday I was
Killing myself slowly,
Letting him control
Me completely like a fool.
Never imagining I could possibly
Overcome the
Past twenty-four years of pain I have been in,
Quietly
Relapsing over and over again.
Suffering for
Too Many Years,
Unable to let go.
Voices in my head,
Whispering to starve myself slow.
Xclaiming from happiness,
Yet ashamed that I'm in pain.
Zero is the magic number Ed wants me to weigh.

Written By: Autumn

Autumn Christ

My Journey Through Recovery

My eyes are dull in these shadows;
Your clouds hold an impervious weave.
Just tell me, "When will there be light?"
Or, "How long must my heart grieve?"
Unawakened, unscathed by tremulous fear,
Restlessness becomes my sleep.
No one sees the pain that crouches and hides, in
Each downward glance that I keep.
Yearning, screaming, trapped from my life,
Tears sting against familiar cheeks.
Hear me–please, won't you hear me?!
Reveal now: *the body that speaks*.
One lonely girl, broken and scarred,
Unsure where this falling will land–
Giving her last breath, she lifts up her eyes.
Hope opens the palm of its hand.
Reaching to capture this wave–a sweet savior,
Emptiness groans at my side.
Coldness creeps o'er these soft pearly bones,
Only, this time, I'm warmed by the tide.
Vibrancy still bleeds in dullness.
Each day holds not its own plan.
Real living still comes to me pieces by pieces,
Yet I'm learning now just who I am.

Written By: Kristie McKonly, 16

Her Picture

I found a picture in my box,
Hidden by hundreds more.
The dazzling photo caught my breath,
I met this girl before.
Clothed in a gown of satin and silk,
She held my eyes forever.
Light spilled upon her beautiful face;
Smile lit brighter than ever.
Set flowing against her flawless frame,
Was an illuminating gold.
Each sparkling piece above her chest
Reflecting light as they were told.
Beyond this dress was something more,
What pulled me from the start.
Her figure, her eyes, this pretty girl
Completely stole my heart.
Mesmerized in her perfection,
I couldn't help but count the ways.
My hand took to her every line;
An unexplainable maze.
Endlessly long and narrow,
Her shape was nothing more.
This trail of elegant thinness
Began along the floor.
Though her legs were covered in golden sheen,
The shadows spoke their story.
Moving along, just inches above
Was all that held her glory.
Her fingers fell below her hips,
Each delicate, soft and long.
The sharp curve of hipbones seized my stare,
Now fighting to be strong.

Autumn Christ

With a waist so small and tiny,
You could place your hands around.
My finger traced her further,
Unsurprised by what it found.
A sea of shoulders, chest and neck
Defined in waves of bone;
Little features detailed in her smile,
Thin, too; I should have known.
Her deep brown eyes stared into mine,
My heart stopped in its place.
Dropping the picture, I covered my mouth.
Tears ran down my face.
I was having trouble breathing;
My chest couldn't take the pain.
The girl now lying on the floor,
Will never look the same.
She's the same girl who is crying,
Yes, that pretty girl was me.
Now she's gone, but I'll never forget;
Memories won't let me be.
I'll remember the touch of each bone and curve;
It hurt but was worthwhile
Now the little girl who lit up a picture,
Can barely fake a smile.
If I could step through that photograph,
Slip in those silver shoes;
To be draped in gold and thin again
There'd be nothing there to choose.

Written By: Kristie McKonly, 16

    Kristie is one of my dear friends I have met through my recovery in the Hershey Medical Center's Partial Program. I thank you Kristie for your beautiful poems you have offered for this book. Please know that I believe in you and know you will recover. I thank you for being my friend. God Bless and thank you for being an inspiration to me. You helped make this book possible.

    ~Autumn~

Letters

The next pages are filled with letters that have been written by those who suffer with Eating Disorders, Abuse Survivors, Self-Injury and Psychological Disorders. You will find that there are some from their families as well. Several of us often write letters to our loved ones trying to help them understand what we are going through then decide not to show these letters to the person intended. The reason for this is because some of us believe that it will only cause more pain or just cannot be understood unless the person we write the letter to is going through what we are dealing with.

The letters from family members and friends also show us the other end of the spectrum. How they deal with our pain, what they feel themselves about how we are torturing ourselves and how much these disorders hurt them knowing we are going through these daily battles within ourselves. Some letters are from my family and ones I have written to them also, yet have never been seen until now. Our guilt when we go through these times tend to make us avoid what we would normally do or say.

This chapter is very important because you are going to see both sides of these disorders not just how you the sufferer or survivor is feeling, but how others feel and the fear they have for us wishing it would all go away. You can feel the love, pain, trauma, loneliness, emptiness, anxiety, fear and the tears that are cried in these letters. Please read them carefully as someone you know may be relating to you more than you realize and you may have no idea just what you mean to someone who loves you until it is too late.

If we could take away the anger, frustrations and screaming we do out on paper rather than each other when it comes to these disorders, maybe we could find a way to heal and not be so judgmental against one another believing that there is simply no hope in sight. God Bless.

Autumn,

Here are some of my heartfelt feelings of your dreadful disease, your eating disorder. It's amazing how we have become such fast friends after meeting you the first time. At first you were very bubbly and vibrant, then one day you became so depressed and that was the beginning of my witness to your battles with yourself.

We got you to start eating a quarter of a sandwich and I was elated to see you bounce back a little. Every time I though you had found your utopia once again you would fall. I remember quite well the day I told you that I was going to prepare myself for your death. As you recall, I cried so hard that day. I hate the times when you are on top of the world with the way your life is going and all of a sudden it's nothing but hell once again.

I never had a daughter, but I sure found one when you came into my life. Many times I wish that I could slap you in the face or snap my fingers and all would be fixed. I pray for you each and every day and my greatest wish for you is that someday you will find your higher power and believe in that with all of your heart and soul.

Thank you for accepting me as your "Mama" it is truly an honor.

Peace and Love,

Marjorie

(Mama)

Autumn,

I sat here with the intention of spewing out all the crap that Mama and I have gone through trying to understand the cunningness of the monster that lives within you. That beast that has caused you to lie and to deceive us when it came to the purging and laxative abuse. But instead, I am going to say that we love you more than just words can say. Also, I want to commend you on the great effort you have put forth in attempts to kill that monster. We have been here for you through thick and thin over the past couple of years and we will be here for you forever.

I had to make myself believe and realize that there isn't really anything we can do to help you except to support you in your fight. We have seen you at your best and your worst since you walked into our lives, and there is still love her for you.

The undertaking of this book is surely about the most important thing you could have done to help yourself heal. Believe me, we are so proud to see the glow returning to your skin and that light in your eyes. Let this book be the salvation for yourself and anyone else out there who is battling their own private dragons.

What you need to see is that beautiful person living inside you, and not what you believe the mirror is showing you. Autumn, continue to work on your recovery, remember I know what recovery is and the struggle it takes to stay strong. With love for yourself and those around you, God will see you through this thing. It is really tough climbing the rough side of the mountain. But with faith, God will see you down the other side.

May God Bless you and keep you with love. We love you.

Mama and Pop Pop

Mama and Pop Pop,

I have never been able to share with you the pain that I live in everyday of my life. I have told you about the reasons my eating disorder and depression exists, but to open up completely and share my innermost pain cannot be done. I am afraid I would cause you too much pain knowing you love me so much and want me to be happy. I know it hurts you when I am hurting so I just keep it all inside. It is the best for all of us concerned I guess.

Living with Ed is so hard when you know you can let someone else have control of you like I have let so many others in the past have over me. Ed is one of my personalities I guess you could say. He is my protector, my keeper and my best friend. He keeps me safe when others try and hurt me he will come out and stand up for me. He is my knight in shining armor. I have counted on him since I was nine and he has never lead me wrong. I have been thin when I needed to be and never weak around food.

I know that sugar and fat is bad for me and because Ed protects me he doesn't allow me to eat these things. I know in the past two years you have seen the worst and best sides of me and you love me either way no matter what, but sometimes when you believe you are seeing me Ed is really the one you are talking to. He is very manipulative and can lie well, too well in fact.

I am sorry that he does this to you by building up your hopes and dreams for me but he is watching over me and he just won't leave. I have relied upon him for so long that I don't think I will ever be able to let him go completely, I have been working on leaving him for so long and with your love and strength it is getting easier, but any day now I can see him trying to come walking back in.

I am four months into my recovery now and I feel so happy and content with who I am. I want this to last forever and make you both proud of me, I just hope that I do have the strength to continue to fight against Ed. I want you to know that I have not lied to you one time in the last four months of my recovery and Ed has not been manipulating you. He has been watching and listening to everything we say and do and knows he is up against two of the strongest people in my life. I hope he is scared and fears you as much as I love you both. If he does, I know I can win because I love you both just as much as I love my Mother.

Thank you for being there with me through this fight and I pray that I can stay strong and continue this fight against him. I beg of you that if I do relapse you will still love me though, because I could not live knowing you hate me and thinking I was too weak to make you proud of me. I am so afraid of your disapproval in ways I have never been scared of anyone or anything before.

I love you both and will never forget what you have done for me and all you mean to me. Please believe me when I say on my weakest of days I find the strength to fight because I know how much pain I would cause to you both, my Mother and Charles. I guess in some ways I still feel like I have to be perfect and if I am not I will lose you all forever this time.

I have failed so many times before, I couldn't begin to love myself again if I hurt any of you one more time. I hope you can understand that I am still out of control in many ways, but I am trying to be what and who everyone would like me to be. I just don't know if I will ever know who or what I really am myself.

I Love You Both,

Autumn

(Your Daughter)

At one time, I had the "George Carlin" outlook on Eating Disorders. For obvious reasons, I can't repeat it verbatim. But my thoughts mirrored his. After meeting someone with an eating disorder, my outlook has drastically changed. Being in an everyday relationship and seeing things first hand has opened my eyes to a lot of things.

A little about me, I was brought up in a world that was pretty much black and white, with no grey areas. Pretty much hardcore with little compassion for such things as eating disorders and addictions. Myself, I ended up with an addiction and I was able to recover from it. While dealing with my addiction, I realized that there were other factors that contributed to it. Some emotional, some mental.

There is an old saying, "With age comes knowledge" and with me, it rang true. Now that I see things in a different light, I am able to put myself in someone else's shoes. It is very common for people to say "Stop" and ridicule, that is ignorance. Everyone with an eating disorder knows that what they are doing is damaging and hazardous to their health.

An alcoholic knows that drinking and driving can be deadly, yet he still does it. Logic huh. It doesn't make sense. Compassion and understanding is what starts the process to recovery. Yet, it begins with one person. The one with the disorder or addiction has to finally open their eyes and admit the problem exists. In doing so, the next step is to acquire the knowledge it takes to overcome.

A wise man once told me "A real man can admit when there's a problem". That statement rings true. It's a must and it is the hardest step to take. Realization of that begins the journey to recovery. For me, I was scared to do that, yet I did it. After doing this, I understand the causes of my addiction and began to sort out the garbage in my head. Now over ten years later I still grapple with things from the past, yet I stay clean.

Having gone through what I have, gives me the tools to help my Fiancé. It is an everyday struggle. Some days good, some days not so good. But persistence is what will bring better days. My Father has a saying, "Don't give the Pricks the pleasure". What do you expect from a Retired Marine? Simplistically it means, let no person or thing keep you from

Autumn Christ

being happy. Eating Disorders, like Alcoholism, can be conquered and it starts with one person, you!!!

Written By: Charles

My Loving Fiancé

Charles,

I know we have been through so much in the past two years together and you have been there for me through it all. Through three surgeries and having to share me with another man named Ed is more than I could ever imagine putting you through and more than you've deserved. I have never tried to hurt you or lie to you. I have never wanted to be anything but the perfect woman for you. From keeping the house clean, making dinner and cooking well to being the best friend, lover and companion, you have ever had. I have been less than perfect at times in every category and I wish this never had happened.

I have lied to you and I have doubted you as well as your love for me many times. I want to apologize to you for all of this and I hope that you can forgive me and believe that I am trying very hard through my recovery to make you proud of me. I want to earn all of your trust and love back without the fear of giving in to Ed again. I am honored to have you in my life and I wish none of what we have went through had ever happened, but at the same time I think that it all has helped us become closer and make our love stronger.

You have always given me respect and unconditional love that I know I have never deserved, but I am blessed to have your love and I will do my very best to be a better woman to you from this day forward. We have other circumstances that make things difficult, but I know that they will work out as well in time. I just want us to be happy and share a beautiful life together. I know my faults and I will work on them, but know that though we share such a beautiful love together, I still have an emptiness inside me that no one can fill.

Being unable to give us a child naturally kills me inside and I don't know how to get over the loss of this part of our lives together. I feel so hollow and lonely knowing that I will never have morning sickness, cramps, cravings and labor pains. I would give anything to have these experiences. I have you though, and I have your son as my Stepson. Knowing you are willing to be by my side through this time and be willing to adopt children with me and love them is truly the best gift you could ever give to me.

Autumn Christ

    I love you my darling and I know that you are the one for me to share the rest of my life with. I am proud to call you my Fiancé. I know we will spend our best years to come filled with the greatest love either one of us will have ever known. I will never betray you or cause you not to trust me again. I promise you.

Loving You Always,

Autumn

(Ladybird)

Children

Children are born with the innocence and beauty of a blossoming flower in Spring. They never see race or color, what we weigh or how we look, they simply love us unconditionally for who we are and how we treat them. These behaviors are taught and learned based on how they are raised by us, by other children in their early years in school and by what society shows them to be right or wrong. These circumstances and examples will determine who they will become as adults. Body image just like prejudice and hate is taught not natural behavior.

In school kids can be cruel and at home if we are not careful can be just as bad if not worse because we know better. We know the right and wrong ways to act and treat others and if we don't send the right messages to our children who will? We are society and society is cruel.

When there is a so called "chubby" child in their classes at school, it seems they are immediate targets just as the "mentally or physically challenged" are. I know this to be a fact because I have suffered through it when I was in kindergarten until high school. I was tormented throughout school because of my kidney disease and the problems I had because of it. I was called names that were very hurtful even though I knew it wasn't my fault I was born with my kidney problems and I could not change them.

Once the jokes and name calling got old from my kidney problems, it went to being called fat and other harmful names. Why? Because I had become the target of the school. I look back on my younger days now and see pictures from school and realize I was never fat, not even chubby. I was perfectly normal, but because of this my eating disorder developed by the age of nine years old.

I will spend my life teaching the children I share my life with the correct way to treat others. We must show them that respect, dignity, confidence, self-esteem, moral values and honesty as well as trust is the appropriate way to be in life. "Do unto others as you would have done unto you." This is the best rule and guideline we can teach them in their lives.

My Stepson and Niece are two of the most important people in my life and I will never allow them to treat others as I have been treated. My Stepson's parents have done a beautiful and wonderful job raising him thus far and I am honored to now share a part in his life and help him as well.

If we were to see ourselves through the eyes of innocent babies and children our poor self-esteem and body image would cease to exist. Why as adolescents and adults are we so hard on ourselves, yet babies and children we see as perfect little angels even when they have baby fat on them. They are simply adorable and precious this way and we wouldn't change them for the world. So why do we hate and judge ourselves this way. Our best and most important qualities are defined by who we are and how we treat others. We are not defined by how we look. Our minds and souls signify what kind of person we are. We are so careful and concerned with how we treat and raise our children, have we forgotten those same rules apply to us as adults?

Because we have lost our childhood innocence and rather than blossoming into strong and free willed individuals, we grow into angry, hateful and betrayed or harmed adults. What happens to us when we are children if we have been traumatized does affect us in some of the worst possible ways. We must break free from the pain and anger we hold inside our souls before we can begin to heal and show others the true meaning of life, happiness and trust.

Infertility

There are several forms of infertility out there. Believe it or not Eating Disorders are a cause as well. I suffer from Endometriosis. This is very common amongst adolescent women. I know that in some cases it is treatable and infertility won't be a factor. For me I am on the other end of the spectrum and it is not treatable. Not only do I have Endometriosis, but I also suffer with severe pelvic pain, amenorrhea and infertility. I had surgery twice for this and now my only recourse may be having a full hysterectomy. How I got this, just unlucky I guess, but I do have my suspicions. I have lived my life with only one dream and that was to be a Mother, now I must face facts that biologically this may never happen. I am now finding ways to cope with this horrible reality and move on to adopting children in the next year or so.

I always wanted to have twelve children of my own, now I pray for the miracle of just one baby boy or girl to have naturally and be my blessing. Knowing this most likely will never happen. I know there are millions of children who need to be adopted and so I am going to do just that, adopt as many of them as I can to give them a happy, loving, secure and successful life. Together with my Fiancé, we will give them all the love, attention, respect, loyalty and the best in the world possible. They will never want for anything especially unconditional love. This will come from the start and be there eternally for them.

If you are unable to have children in your life, please never stop believing there are children out there for you, because there are. They may not biologically be yours but you can love them just as much and they will grow to love you the same way. Take the time and find him or her and if you choose to have more than one. In fact, adopt as many as you feel you can handle loving and taking care of. They will forever be grateful to you. God blesses us in many ways we don't understand maybe for us who cannot have children of our own, our blessings are out there waiting for us to have through adoption. I know mine are and I thank the Lord everyday for giving me this opportunity to find my little miracles.

Special Thanks

I would like to take this opportunity to give a special thanks to some very special people individually. First of all my Mother, she has done her best to give me everything I could ever need or want in my life. She is there for me whenever I need her and gives me the unconditional love I need. She is my best friend. To my Aunt Shirley who always supports me, loves me and tells me when I am doing wrong. I love you. A special thanks goes to my best friend Leonard for always being there for me and standing by me through all my decisions right or wrong.

To my Mother and Father-in-law, I want to thank them for accepting me into their lives as they have because the have made the last two years of my life much easier. They have been tough as nails on me when I have needed it and have loved me so dearly I could never ask for anything more from them.

To my second Mother-in-law, you have seen me for who I am without judging me based on others in your past and you have not listened to others' opinions about who I am as a person. I would like to thank the rest of my in-laws for finding out who I really am and accepting me as well as giving me advice for recovery.

To my Fiancé, you have supported me through my worst of times and have given me respect, trust and love that I have never known before, even when there have been times it wasn't deserving. Thank you for your love and

I look forward to spending our lives together being husband and wife one day. I also want to thank you for allowing me to be your son's Stepmother, you know how much he means to me. I love you both eternally.

I would like to thank the staff at Hershey Medical Center in Dr.Levine's office for being so wonderful to me. You have dealt with me and continuously tried to help me even when I have been the worst patient and would not accept my eating disorder or health issues. You continued to fight to help me become the healthy person I am today. God bless you for all you have done for me and continue to do.

Finally Christine Mercer-Vernon for her beautiful and inspirational art work which has been illustrated throughout this book. I want you to know how much you have shown to us in the Partial program. You have brought beauty and sunshine into our lives. We have been so blessed to have you in our lives to share in the light and strength you have within.

I dedicate this book to all of you who have an Eating Disorder, have survived Abuse and Self-Injury as well as Mental Illnesses. I wish you all the best in your recovery and strength and I can only pray that I was able to touch you in some small way to help you want to heal and recover. I know how difficult life can be, but together we can overcome our deepest problems.

I would like to offer this book in dedication to the loving memory of Karen Carpenter and her family. I Know how much you loved her and please know she will never be forgotten. She is a precious angel watching over all of us and her memory is not in vein. She is soaring with the angels we have all lost in our lives and will be cherished eternally for her beautiful personality, smile, love, laughter and music. I am truly honored to be a lifetime fan of hers. God bless you all.

Thank You Partial and IOP

This special thank you goes to the patients at Hershey Medical Centers Partial Hospitalization and IOP Programs. You have helped make this book possible. You have inspired me to write this book and give me the desire to heal and help others. Getting to know each and every one of you by spending time together in group has made every difference in my life. I learned something from and about every one of you and I am honored to say I know you on a personal level. I hope we can become friends and keep in touch because I value what we have shared.

The laughter, tears, pain, fears and dreams. I also dedicate this book to you and your recoveries so you may have new and bright beautiful lives. You are blossoming flowers and I hope this book helps you to grow. A person is only as beautiful on the outside as they are on the inside and believe in me when I say you are all the most beautiful people in the world. I thank you from the bottom of my soul for your contributions and you will never be forgotten. I am in my recovery because of you and I only hope I can inspire you to heal as you have inspired me. God Bless you all and remember "Strength Comes from Healing."

In Loving Memory

This book is also dedicated in loving memory to the following people I have had the honor to gain wisdom and love from in my life. You will eternally be loved, cherished and admired for teaching me a special gift about life.

To my Great Aunt Punkin, Aunt Donna, Uncle Jim, Great Aunt Margaret, Grandmother Eva and Aunt Glenda. You have taught me honesty, strength, trust, compassion, kindness, emotional security and unconditional love. You have all made a difference in my life in a tremendous way.

I will forever be grateful to you for loving me as you did and for teaching me so much about how to be a better person. You are my heros and I love you always.

Author's Note

Writing this book has been quite an adventure for me. Not only has it been a success in accomplishing one of my lifetime goals which was to write a book, but also finding a way to help others in need who suffer from Eating Disorders, Abuse, Self-Injury and who have Psychological Disorders. Throughout my life I have learned how hard it is to overcome these obstacles and to know that others are struggling too makes me feel as if there is something I can do to help. This book is my contribution to other survivors of these disorders as a way for them to find treatment and receive help just as I have done. This is why I am donating a percentage of the proceeds from this book and the ribbon awareness campaign I started to Hershey Medical Center and hospitals who have specialized programs dealing with these disorders. The money will go towards helping those in need who do not have medical insurance so they may receive medical care.

Since my first year, I have been fortunate to have medical insurance for my kidney disease, stomach problems, eating disorders and other medical conditions I have had in the past and presently continue to have. If I can help just one person to receive the medical attention they need to help them heal, then my mission in life is near completed. The other part of this mission is to adopt children of different ages and be able to give them the love and attention they have been longing for and desperately deserve.

Our paths are chosen for us by a higher being and for me this higher being is God.

No matter what cards I have been dealt in life, I have found my strength and courage in him to make it through the toughest times. I thank the Lord for blessing me with the path he has chosen for me to lead. Through the worst of times I have found my inner strength, esteem, morals, values and integrity. If you would like to get in touch with me please feel free to do so at anytime by emailing me at overcomeyoured@hotmail.com. I also have a website designed to help others who are struggling with the disorders in this book . They offer links to other website's, help line phone numbers in your area, listings of treatment centers available throughout the United States and books on these disorders for sale. The website address for Overcome Your ED is http://overcomeyoured.tripod.com.

Thank you for helping others to receive treatment by purchasing this book in the Fight Against ED. God Bless you and I am eternally grateful for your help. I know the patients who will be receiving treatment will be as well. I hope that we can help each other recover and heal one person at a time and begin to save lives rather than lose them to these horrible diseases.

Sincerely,

Autumn

A Brief Perspective from a Therapist

I have had the pleasure over the past seven years to work with females who have been diagnosed with eating disorders and many of whom also have had some form of trauma in their pas and/or present lives. I feel safe in saying that they have given me much more than I have given them. These women are some of the strongest people I have ever met. They have been through so much in their lives and have to show an amazing amount of trust to come into treatment and reveal their stories.

I would like to share some of the wonderful things that I have learned in my work with these women:

1. Humans can withstand an amazing amount of abuse and find creative ways to cope.

2. It is an honor to be trusted enough to have someone share with you their emotional pain.

3. Never give up, no matter what!

4. Women can learn to form healthy relationships in adulthood, even if they didn't have a caring and nurturing caretaker.

5. Women who have been diagnosed with eating disorders are some of the brightest and most creative people in the world.

This is by no means an exhaustive list, but I think it describes some of the key points that I would like to make. I look forward to many more years in the eating disorders and trauma fields.

Elizabeth K. Hoffman, Ph.D., L.S.W.

(A caring person first and a therapist second)

Postscript

I have been asked to write a postscript to this remarkable book about hope and recovery. I have had the privilege of being Autumn's physician for the last two years and have been able to observe her recovery and transformation. The details of her journey are described movingly in the pages of this book. Over the last ten years, I have had the opportunity to see many moving recoveries: to see young women with severe malnutrition due to anorexia nervosa start to take a few bites of food that leads them on their road to health, to see women with bulimia stop vomiting and using laxatives, to see women hold back from cutting themselves and using other self-destructive behaviors, to see hope in their eyes and life in their faces.

There is no magic to recovery, no magic pill or treatment. The treatments and medicines can be helpful "tools" for the patients, but there is no "cure" as such- just well meaning professionals trying to help. The recovery lies in the patient, herself and the key is compassion. The patient has to learn to develop compassion for herself as a human being. She needs compassion from her family, compassion from us- her treatment team, and compassion from society. Through love and compassion will be the found the strength and courage to stop the self-destructive cycle of the eating disorder and start down a path to balance and health.

And so, I finish with a tribute to Autumn and to all of the strong and courageous women with eating disorders and with a prayer for their health, well -being and happiness.

Sincerely,

Richard L. Levine, M.D.

Professor of Pediatrics and Psychiatry

Penn State College of Medicine

Director of Adolescent Medicine

Director, Eating Disorders Program

Penn State Children's Hospital

Milton S. Hershey Medical Center

About the Author

In her own words, Autumn describes her lonely path of self-destruction from Anorexia, Bulimia, Self-Injury, surviving Abuse and Psychological Disorders. Now seven months into her recovery, she is learning how to find her inner strength and beauty. She wrote this wonderfully inspiring and captivating book for others who suffer from these disorders.

"Hiding In Plain Sight" is one of the best books that has been written on the struggles, pain and the recovery process of these disorders. Autumn has placed her most personal trials and tribulations in this book with the hope of saving other lives, while she continues to heal. Through unconditional love and support she is now living a happy and healthy life full of confidence in herself.

Printed in the United States
27877LVS00005B/259-291